50 Ways to Train Your Cat

STEVE FRANKLIN

Sally Franklin

RINGPRESS

This book is dedicated to my wonderful husband, Steve, and to all the friends, human and feline, who have helped with its production.

RINGPRESS

Published by Ringpress Books Limited,
PO Box 8, Lydney, Gloucestershire
GL15 6YD, United Kingdom.

First Published 1996

ISBN 1 86054 090 2

Contents

Introduction

UNDERSTANDING YOUR CAT

It is now generally recognised that cats are the most adaptable of all pets; they will live equally happily in a large house or in a small apartment, they will be a companion for a large family or someone living alone, and they will co-exist with other animals. The cat is therefore the ideal pet for present-day society.

It is popularly believed that cats are independent creatures and care little for the company of their human owners. However, this is, quite simply, not the case. Most cats do have an independent streak, but they also have an affectionate nature, which can be enhanced by close interaction with their human owner.

The aim of this book is to enrich your relationship with your cat by a series of training sessions. These range from practical lessons that enable you to handle your cat when he is sick or when he needs grooming, to the more spectacular tricks, like teaching your cat to retrieve or to jump through a hoop. Some cats will learn more quickly than others, depending on age, temperament, intelligence, breed, and the skill of the trainer.

All domestic cats, whether pedigree or of indeterminate breeding, have very individual personalities, although with pedigree cats there may be some common behavioural factors peculiar to your chosen breed. There is no such thing as the perfect breed for training ability. If training is an aim with your pet, then choose a cat with personality traits that complement your own personality, aims and objectives.

FELINE CHARACTERISTICS

The domestic cat, affectionately referred to as the moggie in the UK, has been subject to very little interference by man. Although there are wide variations in appearance and temperament, this type of cat is often tabby-marked, shorthaired, round-eyed, round-faced, with a broad skull and short nose. On average they weigh between 7 and 12lbs.

By definition, all domestic cats of indeterminate breeding are individuals, but many come complete with wonderful training potential, providing they have been frequently handled during the early socialisation period. With their hybrid vigour, they are lively, alert, sensitive, loyal and intelligent.

PEDIGREE CHARACTERISTICS

SIAMESE AND ORIENTAL: These breeds can be considered among the more trainable of breeds. They are very demonstrative, affectionate, territorial, inquisitive and active. They tend to be loyal to their owners and they are often vocal as well.

They demand their owners give them their undivided attention.
BURMESE: This breed has some similar personality characteristics to the Siamese and Oriental breeds, but these are honed with an endearing gentle sensitivity and most trusting nature.
PERSIAN: This group includes Chinchillas and Colourpoints (Himalayan), the most gentle of all the cat breeds; they are quiet, placid and most affectionate. The Peke-faced Persian is exclusive to the USA.
SEMI-LONGHAIR: This group, which includes Birmans, Maine Coons, Norwegian Forest Cats, Ragdolls and Turkish Vans, have personalities that are a halfway house between the Persian group and the Burmese, Oriental and Siamese breed groups. They can be more extrovert and out-going than the Persian group, and more serene and peaceful than Burmese, Orientals and Siamese. In the USA this group includes the American Curl and the Semi-longhair Persian
BRITISH, EUROPEAN AND AMERICAN SHORTHAIRS: These breeds are the teddy bears of the feline world. The patient Manx and American Wirehair are included in this group. They have most affectionate natures and are extremely loving to their owners.

THE TEMPERAMENT FOR TRAINING

There are many factors to consider in determining your cat's trainability:
CURIOSITY AND PLAYFULNESS: A cat or kitten that is bright, alert and curious will be ideal for training. The cat should be relaxed in your company.
INDEPENDENCE: Do not worry if your cat shows some degree of independence. A cat's ability to amuse himself can be used to your advantage when training.
AFFECTION: All domestic cats, providing they have been socialised from an early age, have a natural empathy with people, although this markedly differs according to circumstances and environment.
SHYNESS VERSUS FRIENDLINESS: If you placed these two characteristics at opposite ends on a horizontal scale, you might think that you should naturally pick the most friendly cat or kitten. In most cases, this selection may prove to be the best one and you can get him to perform tricks in front of your friends, but the shy cat may still have training potential. Once he gets to know you and trusts you, it is very likely that he will be loyal and loving. It is quite likely that his devotion will make him extra responsive to your training efforts besides bringing him out of himself.
AGE: The age of your cat or kitten does have some bearing on his aptitude for training. Basically, you should not choose a cat that is too young or too old, although there are always exceptions to the rule.
SEX: Gender is not important in choosing your trainee. Both male and female kittens, providing they are neutered, will turn into well-adjusted adults. Both sexes can be trained; one being no better than the other. However, you would probably find difficulties in training an unneutered stud cat. Breeding queens have strong, mothering, protective instincts that may get in the way of training.
HEALTH: A healthy cat is a happy cat, and it is essential for your cat to be in good physical condition before you proceed with any form of training.

INSTINCTIVE BEHAVIOUR

All newborn kittens have a strong instinct for feeding and preservation and this is apparent when watching newly-born kittens blindly struggling over their mother's abdomen to find the choice nipple in the milk bar. Kittens do not have to be taught to suckle to survive, and the maternal instinct of a first-time mother is not the result of a training programme in motherhood.

External stimuli can bring out instinctive behaviour in your cat – the noise of a bird's fluttering wings, the sight, smell and sound of a mouse fleeing for its life, the high-pitched cry of a frog followed by the gentle sound of a splash as it leaps into the sanctuary of its pond. Some cats have an urge to mark their territory with spraying. This sometimes happens in a multi-cat household when the hierarchical order of a group of cats has been challenged.

MEMORY AND REASONING ABILITY

Most cats exhibit self-taught behaviours. For example, a young kitten, for no reason at all, decides to carry a paper ball in his mouth, brings it to you and indicates his desire for you to throw it away for him to retrieve. Other cats suddenly demonstrate their prowess at opening doors and flicking on light switches with their paws.

These self-taught behaviours reveal that cats have some reasoning ability and understanding of cause and effect, a degree of memory that is being reinforced by repeated attempts at the same behaviour, and also some degree of memory retention.

MOODS

Cats, like humans, have moods. All cat owners have experienced the 'mad half-hour', when the cat runs madly around the house without rhyme or reason, knocking into things, running around furniture. Although this form of behaviour can be attributed to mood, there is some indication that it may have its origin in the days when cats were undomesticated and used to have to hunt for a living.

Some owners believe their cats are affected by the changes in the moon, and on nights of full moon some cats appear to be more restless than usual. Again, this has been put down to the pull of the moon's magnetism on the cat's body and brain fluids. We have all seen the advent of hot summer days when cats, like us, tend to become lazy. As the weather becomes cooler, cats become more lively. Moods also affect the success of training your cat.

MENTAL AND PHYSICAL MAKE-UP

The cat's brain is similar in structure to that of the human being, but is at least 30 times smaller in size. A cat has five senses: smell, taste, hearing (including balance), sight and touch, which are finely honed for detecting prey and hunting.

COMMUNICATING WITH YOUR CAT

A cat is certainly capable of communication; he recognises his owner by sight, and he certainly recognises his owner's voice and smell. Dog behaviourists believe that the dog sees their owner as the leader of the pack. A cat, however, behaves differently, resorting to kitten-type behaviour as he rubs his body against your body. Most also remember the instinctive nursing behaviour when their paws kneaded their mother's body when suckling milk.

Some behaviourists believe that the cat sees his owner as a mother figure, and there are many cases of cats pining – and even losing the will to survive – if they are deprived of human affection.

VERBAL COMMUNICATION

Cats are capable of a variety of sounds which are all part of their communication process.

PURRING: All cats and nursing kittens when happy, contented and at peace with the world, purr. No-one quite knows how a cat purrs, but it is thought that this sound emanates from the vibration of a large blood vessel in the chest. When this sound reaches the windpipe and throat, it produces a purr.

MIAOWING: A cat is able to vary the sound of his miaow depending on his feelings or actions. A long, loud miaow can indicate that the cat is upset, frightened or hurt, whereas a chirruping miaow can indicate he has seen a fly on the wall and would like to catch it. A gentle-sounding miaow tells you that all is at peace in his world.

HISSING AND HOWLING: Breed differences play a major part – Siamese cats are well-known for their howls. However, all cats when faced with a strange animal or even another cat, are instinctively hostile until the barriers have been broken down. Hostility is expressed with hissing, and a cat-fight with loud howls, growling and spitting.

BODY LANGUAGE

The body language of your cat can tell you a great deal about how he is thinking and feeling. More importantly, it can tell you how receptive he will be to a training session!

It is no good trying to train your cat to walk on a lead when his ears lie back, his back is arching, his coat is standing on end and his tail is beating against your legs. However, you will know when your cat is content. He will be purring loudly, his ears will be positioned high on his head, his coat will lie flat to his skin, his back will be relaxed, and his tail will be held erect with pride.

There are many other signs of body language and as you and your cat become confident in each other's company, you will soon learn what he is telling you. The interpretation of your cat's body language is one of the most important training tools you have.

THE CAT AS A 'SYSTEM'

When training your cat, it is helpful to think of the cat as a system. The 'output' is the desired behaviour that you want to teach your cat. The 'input' is the instruction, guidance and help that you, the owner, gives. The 'system' is the pathway in the cat's mind that determines behaviour, i.e. the brain of the cat. The conditions for the system need to be considered for each learning situation.

The key point for you, as a trainer to know, is that only an input will produce an output. If you want your cat to recognise your input, you must be consistent: use the same word, voice tone, hand signal each time. If you use a different input, the cat cannot understand what you want.

TRAINING TARGETS

Training your cat starts with deciding what you want the desired output of your cat to be after training. These are called 'training objectives'. For training to be successful, it is best to work on one objective at a time.

For each situation, you need to consider what are the right conditions for your cat to learn. Some of them are obvious, for example, the cat must be happy, healthy and feel secure with you as the trainer. Equally, you have to have the right equipment available to train your cat, and preferably a quiet, undisturbed area for training.

Try to understand your particular cat, as he already has some systems knowledge that you can use in training. For example, what are the food treats that he particularly likes? These are the ideal rewards. If anything frightens your cat, make sure it cannot interfere with training.

For most owners, the main input is a spoken command such as "No", "Sit", etc. Some trainers use external stimuli such as clickers or whistles to reinforce training, so the cat learns to do the desired behaviour to a particular noise instead of voice commands. Other trainers use both voice and external stimuli together.

CLOSING THE LOOP

By now you may have realised that the systems approach is not complete. You cannot just give an input, e.g. the word "Down" and expect your cat to obediently flop on to the floor. In order to learn what response you want to your input, the cat has to have some feedback as to whether he is doing what you want.

You must first decide how to give the feedback. Many human training books talk about a 'stick and carrot' approach to learning, using things people like (carrots) to reinforce positively, and things people hate (sticks) for negative reinforcement. However, for cats, the only relevant approach is the carrot approach. This is usually by food treats and loving, praising behaviour, immediately after your cat realises what you want him to do.

There are times when your cat may need to be admonished, and in this instance, the strongest weapon is your voice. A strong, loud shout of "No" in an angry voice is usually sufficient deterrent, especially if it comes as a sudden surprise – cats generally detest sudden noises. If "No" alone is not enough, clapping hands or hissing can reinforce the point. If all else fails, water is the last straw to a cat. We keep a water-spray handy, and a firm "No" followed by a quick, surprise, squirt of water is usually enough of a deterrent for any of our cats.

The second factor in giving feedback to your cat is repetition. Every time he responds in the way that you want, you must reinforce that this is *good* behaviour. This repetition has to happen every time until he learns, and can then be reduced gradually.

There can be no real timescale for each activity; each cat is an individual and therefore, will progress along at his own pace. All the owner has to do is to satisfy himself that his cat has learned what is expected of him.

In each of the following sections there is some guidance on how to reinforce good behaviour appropriately, but do consider, in each case, how your cat will react. Think carefully about making your message plain throughout the training and your friend will soon learn how you want him to behave.

Chapter One

STARTING FROM SCRATCH

Once you have a cat or cats in your home, it is important to ensure that the cat understands how to behave in your house. This chapter deals with the most important basics to ensure that you and your cats live in harmony together.

1. HOW TO USE A LITTER TRAY

A litter tray and litter are two of the most important components of your cat's life and are essential items if you want your cat to be house-trained. Even if your pet will generally use the great outdoors as his litter tray, it is advisable to start by keeping him indoors until he feels at home in his new surroundings.

Keep the litter tray in the same place but if you have to move it, do remember to show your cat its new location. Many owners keep their cat's litter tray in the bathroom, shower-room or utility room, which makes cleaning easy. Also remember to keep the litter tray out of the way of young toddlers, small children or dogs.

Some cats still have accidents after they have learned to use a litter tray – much to the exasperation of their owners. Accidents are caused by several factors, such as change in location, while others have physical causes or stem from psychological problems. Whatever the cause, do not shout at your cat, as there is a good chance he will reward you with even more misbehaviours. Behaviourists may refer to these problems as 'inappropriate defecation and urination'.

EQUIPMENT: There is a variety of different types of litter tray available, but all have one essential factor: a rectangular-shaped tray with graduated corners, which should be strong and deep enough to hold a 2-3 inch depth of litter. The hooded litter tray is now widely accepted. It varies from trays with basic plastic hoods, to more complex models with charcoal filters, to the most sophisticated of all, an air ioniser which works electrically to reduce odours.

There are many different types of litter on the market ranging from wood-based to clay-based, to minute particles of sponge designed to offer the maximum absorbency. The choice of litter is purely subjective, depending on how you evaluate the absorbency, weight, odour control and tracking factors.

TRAINING OBJECTIVE: To ensure that your cat uses the litter tray and does not have accidents around the house.

TRAINING STEPS

1. Cats naturally look for somewhere soft to use as a toilet, and most kittens start to

use the tray naturally at around 4-6 weeks of age. Some late developers need help. This entails picking up the youngster after he has eaten and gently rubbing his rectum with a piece of kitchen towel, tissue or cloth. It is quite possible that he will urinate straight into it. However, if you quickly follow this action by placing him in the litter tray and gently paddle his front paws in the litter, he will soon start to use the litter.

There are a number of steps that you can take if your pet will not use the tray but messes round the house instead.

2. Confine your cat to a pen where the litter tray contains the only soft material. Confinement means the cat is reduced to eliminating in the litter and, often, this is enough to correct all but the most determined cases.
3. Ensure that any areas where the cat has an 'accident' are fully cleaned and disinfected, and also that any remaining smell is removed. Cats often return to an area guided by smell. There are several proprietary products available to help get rid of any remaining odour.
4. Place your cat's food dish on the spot where he messed (after cleaning of course!). Cats do not like eliminating in an area where their food is available.
5. If the problem persists, have your cat checked by a veterinary surgeon. It is possible that a medical problem has arisen, and this could be affecting the cat's behaviour, or his ability to use the tray.

2. TO USE A CAT FLAP

One of the most useful pieces of equipment to purchase is a cat flap. It will save a great deal of time and energy if you intend your cat to have the use of an outside cat run or garden. Crime prevention officers advise that the cat flap should be situated at least 2 feet away from your door lock.

EQUIPMENT: Cat flaps range from a four-way lockable flap for use in glass doors to a de-luxe type with a tunnel suitable for easy installation. An electronic model (operated by your cat's collar which contains an electronic device) will prevent other neighbourhood cats from sampling your hospitality. Some models come with a lock which is useful for restricting your cat's freedom.

Ideally, the bottom of the cat flap should not be more than 6 inches (15 cms) from the ground to allow your cat to walk through the flap, rather than jumping through it. An average size is 7.5 ins x 9.5 ins, but a cat weighing over 14 lbs may need a larger entrance.

TRAINING OBJECTIVE: To enable your cat to go in and out at will, without having to ask for your assistance.

TRAINING STEPS

1. Prop the flap open, and entice your cat to walk through it by showing him some of his favourite food. Encourage your cat to eat the food reward once he has passed through the door.
2. Repeat Step 1 a few times, until it is obvious that this lesson has been mastered.
3. Encourage your cat to push with his head against the flap to open it, so that he can see and smell the food reward on the other side. Once your cat has walked through the flap, offer him the food reward.

4. Show your cat his food reward again, put it outside the flap and then call the cat to walk through the flap to receive his reward. If you have a dual cat flap, train your cat to walk through from the outside to inside your home. Remember to give plenty of praise, and soon the cat flap will become your cat's preferred method of entry into your home.

3. TO USE A SCRATCHING POST

When a cat scratches his claws, he is not being wilfully destructive. He is sloughing off the dead outer husks and maintaining the claws' sharp points. It is also a means for the cat of stretching and exercising his muscles, particularly when he wakes after a deep sleep. Scratching is also a territorial marking function; a marking scent is released from the glands in your cat's paws.

EQUIPMENT: There are many sophisticated scratching posts on the market including branches covered with leaves, pagodas, and carpeted tubes. Some of these can be quite expensive and, in some cases, cats can reject scratching posts if the surface is not sufficiently rough. A good-sized log can also be used; the external bark should be soft and moist so that it does not splinter or crumble.

TRAINING OBJECTIVE: To ensure that your cat uses a scratching post rather than your furniture to sharpen his claws.

TRAINING STEPS
1. Position the scratching post in a place that is easily accessible, or where the cat has already started to sharpen his claws.
2. Take him to the post, lift his front paws and gently place them on the rope, carpeted or wood surface. Some cats instinctively dig their claws into the post and scratch. Reward your cat with his favourite treat.
3. If your cat does not begin to scratch, gently press his paws to extend his claws and hook them into the surface of his post. Praise him and offer a food reward.
4. If your cat is still reticent in using his scratching post, lightly sprinkle the post with a dusting of catnip – this is one of the few times this mind-bending herb can be used as an aid to training. When buying dried catnip, buy a green herb. If it is white, or dry and dark in colour, it may be old stock.
5. Attach a dangling toy or feathers to the post, or wave a toy or feather in front of the post so that your cat's claws will sink into it as he tries to grab the toy. Do this two or three times to reinforce the training.
6. Encourage movement up or down the post by making your cat chase the toy.

4. TO PLAY WITH TOYS

Toys and a scratching post should be introduced early on, as the kitten, growing in confidence and security, will start to look for items to play with, and will want to exercise his claws. In reality, the kitten is developing his skills and reflexes, in preparation for adult hunting sallies. Playing with your cat helps to build up a strong mutual friendship, and it is essential for on-going training success.

EQUIPMENT: Cats and kittens love toys that move or encourage them to chase and catch. Pet stores, garden centres, supermarkets, and trade stands at cat shows stock an amazing array of toys, many garnished with a sprinkling of catnip. These range from ping-pong balls to large aerobic exercise stands and 'fishing-rod' type toys with dangling balls, snakes and bird feathers. Home-made toys can be equally effective when playing with your cat. One of the most useful toys we have ever made consisted of a stiff, pastic bag placed inside an old sock. A cat will pounce and 'kill' this over and over again.

Play is an essential element of training as your cat will learn to be responsive. Photo: Neil Watson.

TRAINING OBJECTIVE: To train your cat to play with the toys you provide, rather than the tassels on your three-piece suite.

TRAINING STEPS

1. Start by throwing a ping-pong ball or crumpled sweet paper for your cat. Most cats will respond by chasing the toy along the floor, and sometimes they will instinctively bring it back for you to throw again. Sweet papers that have enclosed mints are most popular.
2. If your cat appears disinterested, try using paper tied to a string, or a similar 'fishing-rod' style toy. Draw the end along the floor past the cat, who should then pounce and 'kill' the end.
3. Safe toys, such as ping-pong balls, should be available at all times so that the cat always has an alternative to the household furniture.

5. TO CLIMB A TREE – AND GET DOWN

Cats will often climb a tree for immediate sanctuary if chased by another animal, and sometimes they cannot resist chasing squirrels or birds into the leafy branches. The issue is how to train, or persuade, your cat to climb down.

EQUIPMENT: A suitable tree trunk, a cat harness and lead (optional, for use while training).

TRAINING OBJECTIVE: To ensure the cat knows how to climb down as well as up a tree, thereby avoiding the need to borrow ladders or to call the Fire Brigade for assistance.

TRAINING STEPS

1. Find a suitable tree and encourage the cat to grip the trunk with his claws at your head height. Make sure the cat cannot climb higher! If you are worried about your cat running away during his early training sessions, use a harness and lead for extra security. Now encourage the cat to *back* down the tree, trying to stop him jumping for as long as possible. Repeat, gradually increasing the height, until the cat is used to crawling down backwards, rather than trying to face forwards down the tree (which stops the claws gripping). When your cat has reached the ground, praise and reward with his favourite food treat.

If, despite your best efforts, the cat does get stuck up a tree, try the following:

2. Place a plate of enticing food, such as pilchards in tomato sauce, on the ground where the cat can see it. Leave the area, and, hopefully, the cat will be tempted down.

3. If this does not work, use a ladder, or seek expert help from your local Fire Station. Make sure you have a secure cat carrier in which to place the cat as soon as he is brought down, because the cat will be very frightened.

6. TO LEARN THE CONFINES OF HIS TERRITORY

When you first get your cat or kitten, you must decide whether to let your pet have the freedom of your garden, or whether to confine your cat to the house. There is only so much you can do to train your cat to stay within his boundary. However, you can take measures to ensure that the territory your cat has access to is totally cat-safe.

EQUIPMENT: Optional water-spray, fencing, chicken-wire.

TRAINING OBJECTIVE: To try to keep your cat in the areas you want him to think of as his own.

TRAINING STEPS

1. Spray your cat with the water spray whenever he approaches a door, window, fence or any other 'no-go' area. Say "No" in a firm tone as you spray him to emphasise the undesirable behaviour.

2. Enclose your boundaries. This can be done in a number of ways, such as building an enclosed cat run, attaching an angled wire mesh top to your existing fence, or even electrification (at a safe level) of your boundary. Although controversial, it has been found that the low voltage electrical shock received by a cat attempting to invade your territory ensures that your garden becomes the sole sanctuary of your cat.

3. Fence off any water sources, such as lakes, rivers and streams that course through or edge your property, as they could prove very hazardous.

4. Fix chicken-wire around a tree trunk to prevent your cat from climbing up it and leaping over your boundary fence.

7. TO LEARN HIS NAME

Most kittens can be taught to respond to their names, and your task is made very much easier because your young kitten or cat will have very quickly identified you as his source of food and affection.

TRAINING OBJECTIVE: To help your kitten or cat know his name and be able to distinguish it from other words or cats' names.

TRAINING STEPS

1. Always use the same name whenever you address the cat. Try to decide the name at the beginning, and avoid using other forms or abbreviations.
2. Call out your cat's name clearly, using a high-pitched, chanting tone.
3. If he ignores you, do not offer a treat, and try again. When your cat does look at you, give him a treat and praise him again using his name.
4. When his attention wanders, repeat his name. With luck, he will turn his attention back to you and you can offer him another treat. With repetition, for example, when you are grooming him or stroking him, your cat will learn to respond to his name.

8. TO COME WHEN CALLED

Once your young kitten or cat has learned his name, you can train him to come to you whenever he is required by turning this part of training into a game.

TRAINING OBJECTIVE: To train your cat to come when you want him, in response to your call.

TRAINING STEPS

1. Repeat the training steps used when your cat was learning his name, but this time call from a short distance, such as across the room. Gradually extend the distance until you are calling from another room or from upstairs.
2. If your cat is initially reluctant to come, use a bowl of food or treats to encourage him.
3. Carry a few treats in your pocket when you are in the house. Periodically, call your cat, and he should come running to you to collect his reward.
4. When your cat is responding well, do not *always* reward with food. Make sure you give plenty of praise, and this will soon be sufficient motivation.

Chapter Two

HOUSE RULES

There is a saying that people never own their cats – instead, cats manipulate people. This is not strictly true because owners can instil some sense of home ownership into their cats. When a cat or kitten is first introduced into his new home his initial understanding is that your home is his home, and that he has the freedom to do what he wants, when he wants. His thoughts may not coincide with yours, as you want to protect your soft furnishings and antiques from a cat-assault course. However, a series of basic training exercises will enable you and your cat to live in harmony.

9. HOW TO LEARN NOT TO STEAL

This is one of the areas in which you can greatly help yourself. It is counter-productive to leave a succulent roast chicken on the dining-room table and expect your cat to saunter past with an iron resolve and ignore what his senses and innate predatory instincts are communicating to him.

EQUIPMENT: Optional water-spray, aluminium foil.

TRAINING OBJECTIVE: To prevent your cat from stealing anything you regard as your property.

TRAINING STEPS

1. Keep your cat out of the kitchen or dining area when cooking or eating meals. You are removing the temptation to steal tidbits, besides acknowledging safety and hygiene factors.
2. Train your cat not to jump on to kitchen surfaces or tables to steal tidbits. This can be achieved with a well-directed squirt from a water pistol, accompanied by a loud, firm "No". Do not let your cat see you aiming with the water pistol as you could frighten him. Remove your cat immediately from the surface. You need to be consistent with this form of training to reinforce your point.
3. Extra diversionary tactics can be implemented by covering the work surfaces with aluminium cooking foil so that if your cat jumps up when you are not around, he will be immediately deterred. All cats dislike this shiny, slippery surface.

10. NOT TO SCRATCH FURNITURE

Cats that have the run of the outdoors find that nature has provided a wide range of scratching materials. However, many cats are kept indoors and need to be trained to respect your belongings if both of you are going to co-exist happily together.

EQUIPMENT: Optional – claw-clippers, scratching post, water-spray, aluminium foil.

TRAINING OBJECTIVE: To transfer your cat or kitten's scratching skills on to a more cat-orientated surface, and to prevent damage to your home.

TRAINING STEPS
1. Trim your cat's claws on a regular basis. (See Chapter 3.)
2. Provide an adequate cat scratching post or play centre, and train your cat to use it in preference to your own furniture. (See Chapter 1.)
3. Arm yourself with a water pistol or water spray. Use this as a method of disciplining your cat when he scratches any home contents you regard as sacrosanct. As you spray him with water, say "No" in a loud, firm voice. Then, take your cat to his scratching post and encourage him to use it.
4. Cover and tie any forbidden surface with aluminium cooking foil or plastic carpet runner, used the pointed side up. Double-sided sticky tape is also useful for sticking to forbidden surfaces. Cats have an intense dislike for this type of surface.
5. Wipe wooden furniture with cotton-wool balls soaked in lemon grass oil or any other form of citrus oil. Pin fresh portions of orange peel on to furniture fabric. Citrus-based aromatherapy oils are nature's 'turn-offs' to your cat. One word of warning: use a non-seen area of your furniture or soft furnishings to test these products and make sure they do not cause any damage. If you are in any doubt, a liberal application of scented wax polish is also a useful deterrent.
6. Some cats scratch and damage home contents purely because they are bored. If you are out at work every day and cannot spend sufficient time entertaining your cat, think about obtaining a suitable companion for him.

11. NOT TO CLIMB CURTAINS

Cats are often tempted to jump up and climb curtains. Successful training to achieve correct behaviour can be achieved by using the water pistol or water spray in conjunction with the use of the word, "No".

Some trainers make a diversionary noise when the cat is carrying out the negative behaviour by using a clicker in conjunction with the command of "No". A rolled-up newspaper, smacked down on another piece of furniture, provides an additional but useful noise diversion tactic. However, this is not for a cat with nervous tendencies.

EQUIPMENT: Water-spray, clicker, rolled-up newspaper.

TRAINING OBJECTIVE: To prevent your cat from climbing the curtains.

TRAINING STEPS
1. Trim your cat's claws on a regular basis. (See Chapter 3.)
2. Protect your curtains by enclosing them from the bottom upwards in polythene covers or bags. Tack the edges of these bags to hold them in position. Cats dislike the feel of polythene under their pads.
3. Further deterrents, in the form of citrus-based aromatherapy oils or citrus peel segments, can be wiped over the polythene covers.
4. Choose curtain material or nets with a weave that will hinder any climbing tactics. Cats find it difficult to climb curtains made of a smooth and silky finished material.

Start off by using food rewards and soon your cat will learn to use a cat flap, enabling him to go in or out whenever he chooses.

Photo: Neil Watson.

Teach your cat to use a scratching post, rather than sharpening his claws on your furniture!

Photo: Steve Franklin.

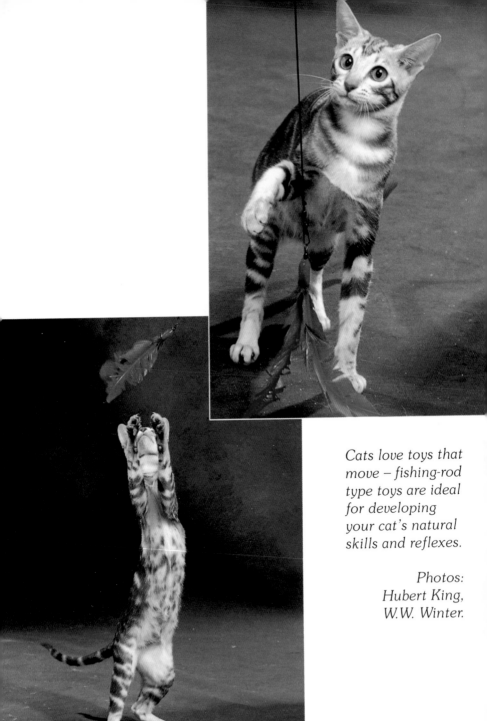

Cats love toys that move – fishing-rod type toys are ideal for developing your cat's natural skills and reflexes.

Photos: Hubert King, W.W. Winter.

ABOVE: It is important to teach your cat to learn the confines of his own territory to prevent him straying too far from home.

BELOW: Kittens cannot resist a game, but climbing curtains is not to be encouraged. *Photos: Steve Franklin.*

CLIMBING BLIND
NEW UNIVERSAL
NEW UNIVERSAL
1974
1975
A-K

ABOVE: Cats will live together happily, providing you spend time integrating the newcomer into your household.

Photo: Neil Watson.

FACING PAGE: A cat will treat your house like an adventure playground, unless he is taught that there are no-go areas.

Photo: Kevin Clarke, Raymonds Photographers.

RIGHT: With careful supervision, a sense of mutual respect can be established between cats and dogs. Photo: Carol Ann Johnson.

FACING PAGE: It is important to train your cat to get on with the younger members of the family. Photo: John Sellers.

BELOW: This pair have learnt to live alongside each other, but it is wise to house a caged pet in a part of the house that your cat does not frequent. Photo: Shaun Flannery.

Your cat can be taught to clean himself by smearing some chicken-stock on his front paws.

Photo: Hubert King, W.W. Winter.

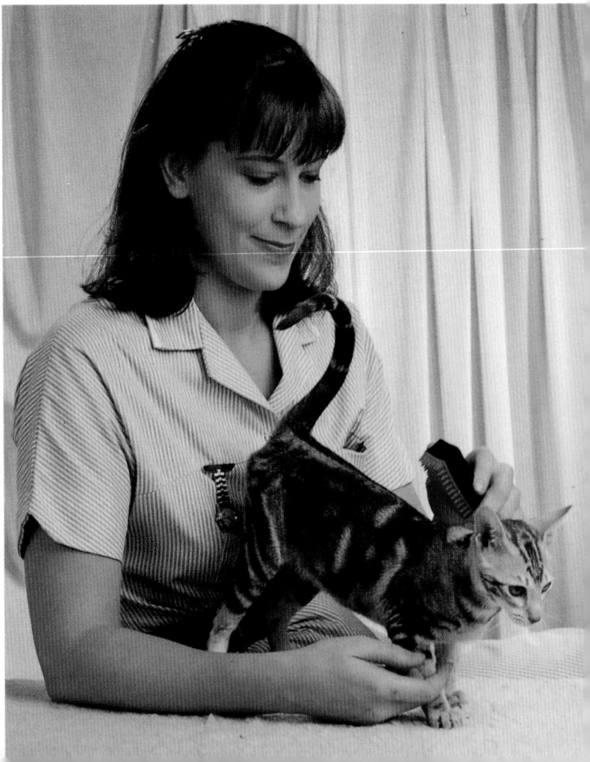

If you accustom your cat to grooming from an early age, he will learn to enjoy the attention.

Photo: Hubert King, W.W. Winter.

12. TO GET USED TO THE VACUUM CLEANER

Most cats and kittens view the vacuum cleaner as a natural enemy, which is hardly surprising as this electric monster usually has a noisy motor. Most cats particularly dislike the upright version, as it appears more menacing, and sets off vibrations on the floor with its beaters. Most cats will never like the vacuum cleaner, but they can learn to live with it.

EQUIPMENT: Vacuum cleaner, kitten pen.

TRAINING OBJECTIVE: To train your cat not to be frightened of the vacuum cleaner.

TRAINING STEPS

1. If you have a pen available, place your cat inside, and vacuum around the pen and in other parts of the room.
2. Repeat Step 1 three or four times until your cat appears relatively relaxed.
3. If you do not have a pen, put your cat in the room while you are vacuuming. If he shows undue distress, let him out of the room. Hopefully, after three or four short exposures to the noise and movement of the machine, he will learn to ignore it.

MAKING FRIENDS

Cats are naturally sociable animals, but they can also form strong hate-relationships if introductions are wrongly handled. Later in this chapter we look at how to help cats form good relationships with other cats, other pets, and with children and babies.

13. TO GET ON WITH OTHER CATS

You cannot put two cats, who have never seen each other before, into the same room and expect them to strike up an instant friendship. However, there are some measures that can be taken to integrate the newcomer. The time it takes to achieve harmony varies, depending on the environment, the age, variety, sex and character of the newcomer. It is often easier to integrate a kitten with an adult; it can take longer with two adults.

EQUIPMENT: Optional – claw-clippers, bedding, treats, cardboard box, kitten pen, fishing-rod toy.

TRAINING OBJECTIVE: To integrate a newcomer into your household in the shortest time, and without any bloodshed.

TRAINING STEPS

1. Clip the cats' claws before first introductions are made. (See Chapter 3.)
2. Cats rely very heavily on their sense of smell, so place your new cat or kitten in his carrier on a blanket that has been used by your existing pet. In this way your pet's coat starts to absorb the familiar smell of your home. Some owners even smear their new arrival's coat with pilchard sauce or similar to encourage the existing residents to lick the newcomer's coat after the introductory period has passed.

3. Supervise early introductions – little and often is the best principle. Make sure there are plenty of bolt-holes available for both the new cat and the existing cats. Open cardboard boxes placed in the room provide temporary bolt-holes.
4. If you have a kitten pen or carrier large enough to accommodate feeding and water bowls, bed and litter tray, place the newcomer inside it during the introduction period. Both new and existing cats will be able to sniff and look at each other without conflict.
5. Feed the newcomer with the other cat or cats in the same room, but using separate bowls placed close to each other. Usually the cats become so engrossed in their food that you can take the opportunity to move the bowls into closer proximity to each other.
6. Stage a play session so that the cats can interact with each other. One of the fishing-rod types of toy is ideal for this purpose.

14. TO GET ON WITH DOGS

Many families accept that keeping a cat and dog together is part and parcel of a normal household; other families would not dream of keeping both pets together. Some breeds, such as terriers, which retain strong hunting instincts, are likely to cause more problems.

TRAINING OBJECTIVE: To integrate a cat or dog into your household in the shortest time, without any bloodshed.

TRAINING STEPS
1. If you introduce a puppy and kitten they will accept each other from the beginning, with the kitten merely hissing at the puppy a few times to show who is boss.
2. If your dog has been used to cats, or the kitten has been brought up with a family dog, there should be few problems. However, they should not be left together unsupervised until you are confident they have reached a mutual understanding.
3. Follow the training steps for 'Getting on with cats', but it is important to be aware that there is a greater risk of injury to either dog or cat, so close supervision is essential.

15. TO RESPECT CAGED PETS

Whatever the background of your cat, whether it is a domestic cat of indeterminate breeding or a finely-bred, aristocratic pedigree, it will retain some innate predatory skills. Even kittens reared in homes with no access to live prey develop the rudiments of predatory behaviour by hunting toys, their siblings or their mother. This behaviour is reinforced in adulthood with housebound cats chasing and pouncing on spiders, fluttering moths or even ping-pong balls.

Cat owners have to accept they cannot train cats to change their instinctive behaviour, but you can take some steps to enable your cat to live in harmony with small animals, such as mice, guinea pigs, gerbils, and with caged birds.

TRAINING OBJECTIVE: To ensure that your other pets do not become part of your cat's diet.

TRAINING STEPS
1. Keep both parties away from each other, in separate parts of the house.
2. There is no conclusive evidence that providing your cat with his daily food will reduce predatory behaviour, as many owners of outdoor cats have discovered. Feeding your cat a large meal and encouraging him to sleep off its effects is only a transient step!

16. TO RELATE TO BABIES
Many couples start life together with a kitten or cat before having a family. Sadly, the advent of a baby can result in the cat being rehomed. Many parents fear that their cat will either sit or sleep on the baby's face causing suffocation. However, with careful thought and planning, it is possible to introduce the cat to both babies and young children and achieve a harmonious household.

Remember, the cat should never be left alone with a young baby or in an area where he may gain access to the child, either through a cat flap or open window or door. This is a rule that should be remembered and applied to newborn babies right through to junior school age children.

If you are choosing a pedigree cat to live in a family environment, it is worth bearing certain breed characteristics in mind. (See Introduction: Pedigree Characteristics.)

HYGIENE FACTORS: Precautions must be taken in pregnancy to avoid picking up the rare, one-celled toxoplasmosis parasite, so, preferably, your partner should take responsibility for the cat's litter tray. If this is not possible, always use rubber gloves, and, after use, wash the gloves and your hands thoroughly. Make sure your cat is wormed regularly. Be very particular about your own hygiene and that of your family when handling pets, especially if you are about to eat or prepare food.

TRAINING OBJECTIVE: To introduce your cat to your baby and achieve a harmonious (and hygienic) household.

TRAINING STEPS
1. Allow your cat to smell the new baby's belongings including both clean and used nappies. This lesson should be repeated on a regular basis over a short period of time. Essentially you are training your cat to realise that the new baby, and its associated paraphernalia and smells, do not represent a threat to your cat's security.
2. Accustom your cat to receiving attention only at your instigation. This must be done before the baby arrives.
3. After the baby's arrival, accustom your cat to receive attention *after* the baby has received attention. This trains the cat to perceive the baby as the prerequisite for receiving his own affection rather than perceiving the baby as competition.
4. Feed the cats and baby separately and, preferably, at different times, from the point of view of hygiene and safety.

17. TO RELATE TO TODDLERS
When your baby begins to crawl, new areas of the house are suddenly available to him. You must guard against the cat feeling or being threatened by a young, mobile infant violating all his known places of sanctuary.

If possible, locate the litter tray in a separate room from those rooms accessed by your crawling baby or toddler. Grooming equipment, small furry cat toys, danglers and scratching posts should also be kept out of a toddler's reach.

TRAINING STEPS
1. Provide sufficient areas of privacy and safety for your cat. Introduction to these areas can be enhanced by sprinkling some catnip.
2. Take your child's hand and show him how to touch the cat without fear to both parties. Show your child how to stroke your cat gently. This introduction, under supervision, trains the child how to communicate with and respect his pet; it also makes the cat aware of the child's right to do so.

18. TO RELATE TO CHILDREN

As the toddler grows into a child, capable of basic reasoning, the relationship between cat and child will change. The young child will find objects at a higher level more interesting, leaving behind his fascination with floor-based objects. He will be more responsive to discipline in the home, and to parental guidance in caring for and handling the cat.

TRAINING STEPS
1. Show your child how to pick up and support a cat correctly. These lessons should be of short duration but on a frequent basis. In this way the child will learn more quickly – and the cat will not be restricted for too long a time.
2. Show your child how to feed your cat. This helps to develop a sense of responsibility and an understanding of the cat's needs. Dried cat food is an ideal product to start with, avoiding the need for a can-opener and/or a knife.
3. Teach your child that a cat must always have access to clean drinking water.
4. Gradually train your child to understand areas of safety and no-go areas for your cat.
5. Leave litter-tray handling until the child is old enough to understand basic hygiene rules.

Chapter Three

CAT CARE

Caring for your cat need not be a one-sided venture. You can actually train your cat to take on some responsibility for his own maintenance, and to co-operate when required.

19. HOW TO WASH HIMSELF

Most kittens are taught from an early age by their mother. The mother is most thorough, licking her kittens in places they cannot reach themselves in early life. She uses her tongue, covered with backwards pointing papillae, which helps with the grooming process. There are times, however, when kittens do not receive this early training, and the owner has to take over. This can occur if the kittens are orphaned or rejected by their mother. It may also apply to a sick cat, who may lose interest in keeping himself clean.

EQUIPMENT: Chicken stock and treats.

TRAINING OBJECTIVE: To assist your cat to groom himself.

TRAINING STEPS
1. Smear some fresh chicken stock on to the cat's front paws, then lift the paw to his nose and mouth so he can smell the offering. This should be sufficient incentive for him to lick his paws clean, which will, in turn, be used to rub the mouth and whisker areas.
2. Extend the smearing of fresh chicken stock on to other areas of the body that the cat can reach.
3. Praise your cat and finish off the training session by offering a favourite food treat.

20. TO ENJOY GROOMING

Although most cats are fastidious groomers, they do need a little help from their owners to be kept in the peak of condition. With so many different breeds of cat, there are obviously many different textures and lengths of coat hair. Longhaired cats require daily grooming between 10 and 15 minutes a day. If this is not done, the long hair can become matted and you will be rewarded with a hole in your wallet as your vet will have to intervene. Shorthaired cats will require the minimum effort in grooming.

EQUIPMENT: There are many grooming implements on the market, ranging from combs with long and short teeth, revolving teeth for longhaired cats and flea combs. Whatever combs you choose, make sure that the teeth have rounded edges as pointed combs can scratch your cat's skin.

Brushes come in all shapes and sizes with natural bristles and synthetic bristles. Static electricity can be generated from a cat's coat with the use of some synthetic brushes. After a few sessions you will decide which areas your cat prefers you to groom first and whether you prefer to use several brushes or combs for different parts of the body. You will also need blunt-ended scissors, treats, and a waste bag or bin for dead hair,

TRAINING OBJECTIVE: To turn the task of grooming into a feline game.

TRAINING STEPS

1. Accustom your cat to grooming as early as possible. It will help if his claws have recently been clipped. Allow your cat to sniff and paw his grooming implements so they do not appear as objects of fear. If his own smell is transferred on to these items it will lessen resistance.
2. Choose your grooming area carefully, and keep to the same area for future sessions. If you change the grooming area frequently, it will only serve to confuse your cat.
3. Comb for 2-3 minutes daily until the cat settles down for longer sessions. While combing him, talk to him in a soothing voice to calm down any agitation he may experience at the beginning. Over a period of a few days you will notice his resistance to being held will slacken as he settles down to enjoy the soothing massaging of his coat.
4. If your cat is *shorthaired*, start grooming on the cat's back, followed by the sides and outer legs. Stretch each leg out in turn to groom the hair around each joint. Finish by grooming the abdomen and tail.
5. If your cat is *longhaired*, use a wide-toothed comb to remove coat tangles. Start by grooming the long hair on the neck and back or, alternatively, the neck followed by the throat area, chest and back. To adequately groom the hair on the neck, you will need to gently tip back the cat's head. Inner thighs can be reached by picking up the opposite leg.

   After combing, locate any matted area found and gently untangle it with your fingers. If this proves impossible, cut off any matted hair with blunt-ended scissors. If the matted hair is too close to the skin, you may need to seek the help of your veterinary practice or grooming parlour.

   Finish the grooming session with your longhaired cat by giving his coat a final brushing. The ruff area needs brushing upwards and outwards so that it will fan his face.
6. Do not pull on your cat's coat, especially if he is a longhaired cat. Your cat will certainly let you know if you are hurting him by either attempting to scratch you, miaowing very loudly or trying to run away from you, which is very counter-productive if you have further training in mind.
7. Reward your cat at the end of each grooming session with an edible bribe, lots of praise and a game.

21. TO ACCEPT CLAW-CLIPPING

A cat's claws are an essential part of his survival kit for gripping and eating food, fighting and climbing trees. They may also be used for grooming purposes.

One of the most important ways of preventing claw damage within the home environment is to regularly trim your cat's or kitten's claws. The act of clipping removes the dead part of the claw, the outer husk, which covers the sharper claw underneath. A cat's claws grow continuously in the same way as human nails. There is no set timescale for maintenance, but a regular weekly check is recommended.

After your cat has had his claws clipped, he may feel the need to scratch the blunt ends of his claws. If you see this behaviour after claw-clipping, transfer him to his scratching post and encourage him to scratch his claws there. Reward him with his treats.

EQUIPMENT: Claw-clippers or human nail-clippers, blunt-ended scissors, treats, a waste-bag or bin for clipped claws.

TRAINING OBJECTIVE: To encourage your cat to accept a weekly manicure.

TRAINING STEPS

1. Pick up one paw and press lightly on the pad to extend the claws.
2. With your free hand, pick up the claw-clippers and place the cutting part over the edge of the claw. When the claw is extended and held up to the light, you will see a pink part within the claw. The pink part is the vein.
3. Trim off the edge of the claw, making sure you avoid the veined area. If you cut into the veined area, the claw will bleed, which will be painful for the cat.
4. Any matted areas between the pads must also be attended to, as this can cause pain to the cat when he stands on his feet. Try to soften the matted areas with water and gently cut them away with blunt-ended scissors.
5. Finish off the manicure session with praise and treats for your cat. If any part of this procedure causes you difficulties, or your cat objects strongly, you will need to seek the help of your vet.

22. TO ENJOY BATH-TIMES

Fortunately, cats do not need frequent bathing, although longhaired cats need more attention, particularly if you plan to show your cat. There is no doubt that adequate preparation beforehand can reduce the trauma a cat may feel. There is no ideal place in which to bath your cat, some owners use the hand-basin in the bathroom, others choose the kitchen sink, while some lucky cats actually have a baby bath bought for this purpose. If you choose the latter, make sure that it is placed on a firm base, otherwise any sudden movement from your cat can upset it.

EQUIPMENT: As well as a bath, you will need: a comb, a brush, blunt-ended scissors, towels, a bath mat, a flannel, a tumbler or jug, shampoo, Vaseline, cotton-wool or cotton-wool balls, a hairdryer, claw-clippers, waterproof apparel and treats. Some of these items can be regarded as optional extras. After bathing your cat a few times, you will know what is required.

TRAINING OBJECTIVE: To introduce your cat to the pleasures of having a bath.

TRAINING STEPS

1. Start to bath your cat at the earliest opportunity. If you are bathing your cat before his first cat show, bath him about 5-7 days beforehand to give his coat enough time to replenish its natural oils and regain its shine.
2. Brush his coat a few hours before you intend bathing him to remove any excess loose hair and dead skin. If your cat has a longhaired coat, check to see there are no matted areas and if so, take appropriate action.
3. Prepare the bathing area and gather the bathing equipment in one place.
4. Clip your cat's claws to reduce the chances of getting scratched.
5. Provide yourself with waterproof apparel.
6. Fill the bath to a depth of about 6 ins. Check the temperature of the water using your elbow.
7. Tear off some cotton-wool, about the size of half a cotton-wool ball, use these as ear-plugs. Remember to talk reassuringly to your cat throughout the process.
8. Wipe a minute amount of Vaseline on the lower lid of your cat's eyes to protect them from water and shampoo.
9. Lower your cat gently into the warm water. If this is his first contact with water, he will probably struggle. Keep calm and reassure him.
10. Wet your cat with water from a tumbler or jug on his back. Let the water flow over his back gently rather than flooding him, which will only frighten him. Avoid his face unless it is very dirty. If you feel you must touch this area, use a clean flannel, wrung out with water to gently moisten his face. If his ears or around his eyes are dirty, these places can be attended to separately.
11. When the coat is sufficiently wet, apply the cat shampoo and lather well. I give my cats two washes of shampoo and use less shampoo second time around, as this wash produces more lather.
12. Rinse the coat, starting with the back first. Make sure that you remove all traces of shampoo, otherwise your cat's hair will have a sticky, clumpy feel to it.
13. Remove your cat from the bath and wrap him in a towel to soak up the excess water. Replace this with another dry towel and towel dry his coat. If you change rooms at this stage, make sure that the new room is adequately heated. If you use a hairdryer to dry the coat, keep it on low volume so as not to frighten him.
14. Reward your cat with praise and his favourite dinner.

23. TO ACCEPT TEETH-CLEANING

A kitten's milk teeth start to appear at approximately 2-4 weeks of age and will number twenty-six. These will be replaced by thirty adult teeth well before the cat is nine months old. The actual age this change takes place varies from cat to cat.

A cat's gums should look pink and healthy. Do not confuse periodontal disease with the black pigment spots that are seen on some cats' gums. Any other deviation of colour or red lines on the edge of the gums, bleeding gums, halitosis (bad breath), or salivating can indicate possible gum disease. Your vet will need to inspect the cat. Other signs of dental problems include weight loss or loss of appetite.

Your veterinary practice will be able to supply the necessary brushes and feline toothpaste. Children's toothbrushes are also the ideal size for cats, and they are probably cheaper to buy. *Never* use human toothpaste on your cat's teeth. It can cause a cat to gag, to vomit or even suffer from digestive upsets. If you are trying to save costs in this area – feline toothpaste is quite expensive – you can make up your own teeth-cleaning solution by diluting baking soda in a little water.

EQUIPMENT: Claw-clippers, antiseptic scrub for washing your hands, toothbrush or whatever you have chosen to clean his teeth, toothpaste, sterilising solution and treats. It may be handy to have a roll of kitchen towel to use to wipe excess paste off his mouth and yourself.

TRAINING OBJECTIVE: To train your cat to accept dental care.

TRAINING STEPS
1. Introduce your cat to a teeth-cleaning routine at an early stage.
2. Make sure his claws have been recently clipped.
3. Wash your hands thoroughly, using an antiseptic scrub, before touching the cat's mouth.
4. Sit the cat on your lap and gently talk to him. Get him used to the idea of you touching his mouth area, lifting up his lip and examining his teeth and gums. Praise him and give him his food reward. Do not forget to wash your hands each time.
5. When the cat shows no fear of having his mouth examined, you can move on to the next part of the training sequence. Wash your hands again, and place the toothbrush in the cat's mouth so that he starts to recognise the feel of it. If he struggles, you may need help to keep him on your lap. It is unlikely that the cat will tolerate the brush for more than a few seconds on the first occasion. Immediately follow up with praise and a food treat.
6. Repeat these sessions until it is clear that placing a toothbrush in his mouth holds no fear for your cat.
7. The next stage in dental training is to squeeze some feline toothpaste on to the brush and place the head of the brush in the cat's mouth. Using a circular motion, brush the outer surfaces of his teeth. You may find it easier to brush from the gums upwards to the tips of his teeth. Talk reassuringly to your cat throughout the process.
8. When your cat shows no fear of this part of the operation, you can tackle the inner surfaces of the teeth. In order to reach the back teeth, you will need to tilt the cat's head backwards and pull his mouth at either side.
9. If there is a build-up of tartar, it can be removed by your veterinary surgeon, if he feels it necessary. This will probably entail an anaesthetic, which, obviously, involves some risk to your cat. If you clean the teeth regularly, you will reduce the chance of your cat requiring dental de-scaling.
10. After each use, your cat's brush can be sterilised by immersing it in a baby sterilising solution, diluted according to the manufacturer's recommendations.

24. TO ACCEPT EAR-CLEANING

A weekly dental inspection and care can be followed by the inspection of your cat's ears. Generally speaking, a healthy cat does not mind his owner holding the ear pinna and examining the cleanliness of the outer ear region.

There are many ear-cleaning items on the market, such as ear-wipes, which are specially treated cloths. You can make up your own ear-cleaning kit by purchasing ear-drops from your veterinary surgeon. Baby oil is also suitable for this purpose. A couple of drops sprinkled on to a cotton-wool ball is sufficient. Make sure you dampen the cotton-wool first so as to prevent any loose strands of cotton-wool working their way into the ear canal. Cotton buds are not ideal for this purpose, as you could cause pain or injury if you probe too deeply into the ear canal.

The excess ear wax you will be removing should be buff-coloured. Any wax that is dark in colour could be indicative of ear mite infestation. If you detect any inflammation or foul-smelling discharge, seek advice from your vet.

EQUIPMENT: Claw-clippers, antiseptic scrub for washing your hands, ear-wipes (or ear-drops or baby oil) cotton-wool balls, rubbish bag and treats.

TRAINING OBJECTIVE: To persuade your cat to sit still and allow you to clean his ears.

TRAINING STEPS
1. Collect all the items you need for this task before washing your hands and picking up your cat.
2. Make sure his claws have been recently clipped.
3. Sit your cat on your knee, and speak to him quietly as you touch his ear.
4. Place the impregnated cloth over your index finger, or hold the cotton-wool ball between your index finger and thumb, and gently hold your cat's ear with your other hand.
5. Using the cloth or cotton-wool ball, gently wipe over the part of the outer ear that is visible. Praise your cat at the end of the session and give him his reward.
6. Clear away the soiled material and wash your hands.

25. TO LIKE DIFFERENT FOODS

Cat owners are faced with an amazing range of different cat diets, and choosing a diet is largely a matter of personal choice. When you have decided which food provides the best diet for your cat, subject to the limitations of your finances, you will need to change your cat from his existing diet to the proposed one without any trauma or diet-related stomach upsets. There may be times when through necessity, your cat has to change his diet, so it is a good idea to broaden his gastronomic horizons.

Some cats will always be resistant to change, and you have to accept that however hard you try to change your cat over to his new diet, your cat will let you know that the old diet is the preferred one.

EQUIPMENT: A variety of feeding bowls, a spoon and a can-opener that are specifically used for your cat's own meals. Some plastic bowls can cause a cat to develop skin sensitivity; stainless steel bowls are very durable and are easy to clean.

TRAINING OBJECTIVE: To turn your cat into a gourmet.

TRAINING STEPS
1. Always use a clean feeding bowl – cats dislike eating from dirty dishes.
2. Mix half the quantity of your cat's existing diet with half the quantity of the new food. If you feed your cat twice a day, use only one-quarter of the daily recommended amount of each food.

When introducing new food into your cat's diet, mix some of the new food in with his usual rations.

Photo: John Sellers.

3. Feed this amount for at least five days so your cat gets used to the taste and texture of his new diet while still being reassured of the availability of his old diet.
4. After the fifth day, slowly increase the quantity of the new diet, on a daily basis, and take out the same proportion of the old diet. By the time you have reached the tenth day, your cat should be switched over to the new diet completely. Praise your cat when he has finished each meal.
5. If you are changing your cat over to a dry diet from a wet diet, do not fill the bowl up with dried food without measuring the amount included. Many owners tend to overfeed dried food; most complete diets only recommend 2-3 ozs a day.
6. Be regular in your feeding habits with your cat. Regular feeding leads to regular elimination of bowels (unless your cat is sick).

Cats are among the most inquisitive of creatures. For their own safety, it is important to discourage them from exploring potentially dangerous equipment, like this washing machine.

Photo: Steve Franklin.

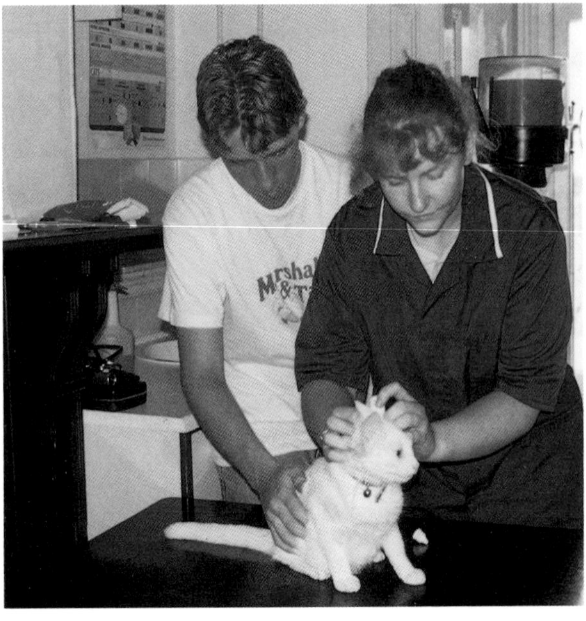

Your cat must learn to accept being handled by a vet, or it will cause major problems if he falls ill and needs treatment.

Photo: Sally Franklin.

26. TO GET ON WITH THE VET

Most veterinary practices deal with a variety of animals but there are some practices that are now specialising in feline medicine. These practices are very much to be treasured as they always attempt to keep abreast of medical developments in the feline world. Ideally, the search for a good vet should commence before you take on a kitten or cat, rather than waiting for an emergency to occur.

Obviously, personalities between owner and vet come into play. Hopefully, you will choose a vet who complements your attitude and feelings towards your cat.

TRAINING OBJECTIVE: To find a feline-friendly vet, and prepare your cat for examinations.

TRAINING STEPS

1. Get your cat used to seeing different people and to being handled by them.
2. Train your cat to get used to his cat carrier. (The steps are covered in Chapter 4.)
3. Choose a veterinary practice based on recommendations and travelling distance.
4. Take your cat on a visit to meet the vet, making sure the cat's claws have been recently clipped. This initial meeting will enable you to assess how your cat adapts to the vet's handling.
5. If this initial meeting goes well, register your cat with the practice.

27. TO BE GIVEN MEDICATION

When they are sick most cats prefer to be left alone to recuperate in peace, but, occasionally, you will need to aid your cat's recovery by giving him tablets and medicines.

Cats often make recalcitrant patients. Like children they are most adept at holding tablets in their mouths, and they object to any cream that has to be smeared on to their bodies. If they have had to be stitched after an operation, they will spend all their recuperative energies in breaking their stitches with their teeth, unless restricted. It is, therefore, important to train your cat to accept medical care, and for you to become adept at administering medication.

EQUIPMENT: Antiseptic scrub, optional pill-popper, plastic syringe, baby sterilising solution, Elizabethan collar.

TRAINING OBJECTIVE: To persuade your cat to take whatever medicine is prescribed.

TRAINING STEPS - GIVING TABLETS

1. Wash your hands with antiseptic scrub and make sure the tablet is readily available.
2. Place your cat on your lap, or on any other firm surface.
3. If you are right-handed, grasp your cat's head with your left hand. Pinch the corners of his mouth with the fingers of your left hand. Pick up the tablet with your right hand, while holding the mouth open with your left hand. Pop the tablet towards the back of your cat's mouth with your right index finger. Allow your cat to close his mouth and gently blow into his face to make him swallow the tablet.

4. Praise your cat and give him his reward of an extra special food treat. Wash your hands after this sequence.
5. If you find you still cannot manage to give your cat his tablets manually, you can try a 'pill-popper', which is available from most veterinary practices. You will need to open your cat's mouth to insert the spring-loaded pill-popper, which shoots the tablet into your cat's mouth. Even though your fingers do not get covered with so much feline saliva, you still need to wash your hands before and after using this implement.
6. Sterilise the pill-popper for further use with baby sterilising solution, diluted according to the manufacturer's instructions.

TRAINING STEPS – GIVING MEDICINE
1. Use whatever measuring device your vet gives you to administer the medicine.
2. Make sure your hands are clean and your cat is sitting on a firm base.
3. When placing the syringe or plastic eye-dropper into your cat's mouth, open his mouth (as detailed above) and gently syringe or drop in small quantities. Allow your cat to swallow between each application. Do not be trigger-happy with the syringe feeder; if your cat receives a very quick and large volume of liquid into his mouth, he may choke.
4. Any size of syringe up to 5 ml is easily manipulated by one hand, anything larger can cause problems.
5. Wash your hands, and remember to sterilise the syringe or dropper after use.

TRAINING STEPS – APPLYING SKIN CREAMS
1. Make sure your hands are clean and your cat is sitting on a firm base.
2. Apply the cream where directed. Talk to your cat for a few minutes to discourage him from licking off the cream.
3. If the cream has to remain on his coat or wound for any longer, use an Elizabethan collar, which is obtainable from your vet, and will prevent the cat licking himself.

After you have carried out whatever medication is needed, praise and reassure your pet. He is probably feeling miserable and will welcome the extra attention from you. If possible, give him food treats, but do not interfere with your vet's instructions on feeding during your cat's illness.

Chapter Four

MAKING PROGRESS

Now your cat has become settled into the household routine, and accepts all members of the family – human and animal – you can start on some more advanced training. In most cases, the training is of direct benefit to the cat, helping him to adapt to different circumstances and situations.

Before attempting any training session, make sure your cat is well and in a co-operative frame of mind. There is no point in trying to train a cat that is tired or off-colour, you will simply build up a pattern of resistance. Contrary to popular belief, a cat does like to please his owner, even if the way he shows it is not as obvious as a dog's would be. Certainly the closer the relationship you have with your cat, the more progress you will make when it comes to training.

28. HOW TO WALK ON A LEAD

This requires considerable patience, and, in some cases, you may find the cat's resistance is difficult to overcome. I have found that a harness is easier to use than a collar, as the cat is more likely to object to pressure around the neck and may well struggle for freedom. However, there are many trainers who have been successful with a collar and lead.

EQUIPMENT: A harness or a collar, a lead, food treats.

TRAINING OBJECTIVE: To enable your cat to wear a harness and walk with confidence on a lead.

TRAINING STEPS

1. Allow your cat to see the harness lying on the floor or chair so that he gets used to its smell and shape. It is likely he will pick it up with his paws and bat it around the room until his attention is diverted elsewhere. If your cat is confident and outgoing, you may be able to ignore Step 1 and proceed to Step 2.
2. Accustom your cat to wearing his harness in the house. Do not be surprised to see your cat rolling around on the floor and looking at you in a very quizzical fashion. He will soon learn to ignore the harness, especially if you praise him and offer him special food treats when you take the harness off his back.
3. Once your cat is accustomed to the harness, attach a lead or piece of string to it, allowing it to trail on the floor as your cat moves around.
4. When your cat finally ignores the lead or piece of string, try coaxing him to move along for a few steps for a few sessions. You can even use a word, such as

"walkies", and train your cat to associate the end of his walk with a "Good boy" and a few treats. The number of sessions you will need to do this will vary from cat to cat.
5. About a week later, your cat should be used to walking on a lead around the living room or wherever he has been trained. Take him out to your garden or to a quiet, safe area, free from traffic distractions, and try a short walk outside. Do not forget to reinforce the training at the end of the walk with treats.
6. After you have accomplished a few walks with your cat and experienced no problems, you can start withdrawing the treats on an ad hoc basis, so that he will come to recognise that a walk is good for his waistline, without adding to it!

29. TO TRAVEL IN A CAT CARRIER

There will come a time when you will have to train your cat to accept being restricted and moved from one place to another within the confines of a carrier. Some cats object to this, whereas others quickly adapt to the confinement and will settle quietly to sleep for the duration of the journey.

Cat carriers come in a range of sizes and finishes. It is important that the carrier you buy is large enough to allow your cat to stretch himself, and also to curl up and sleep if he wishes. Many people start with a cardboard carrier, supplied by the vet. Although this may be sufficient for one journey, most cats will very quickly be able to escape by tearing a way out. A more permanent solution is needed.

EQUIPMENT: A cat carrier, bedding, food treats.

TRAINING OBJECTIVE: To train your cat or kitten to sit comfortably, and without fear, inside his cat carrier.

TRAINING STEPS
1. Introduce your cat to a carrier as soon as possible. Make the inside of the carrier as comfortable as possible with a bed or blanket. Your cat's own bed or blanket will increase his feelings of security.
2. Place some favourite treats at the other end of the carrier and allow your cat to explore the inside confines.
3. Allow your cat to take his own time to enter the carrier. This step should be repeated over a number of days until you are happy that your cat has accomplished his training.
4. Once familiarisation has been achieved, close the door on the cat so that he learns he is restricted. This should not affect him unduly as he will recognise and feel comfortable in his carrier.

30. TO TRAVEL BY CAR

Your cat may need to travel in the car if you are going to the vet, or he may need to travel for longer periods if you are going on holiday or attending a cat show. A cat must never travel unrestrained in a car – it is very dangerous for cat and driver alike. Some cats do suffer from car-sickness. This can be caused by a faint smell of petrol or diesel but, more often than not, it is caused by the motion of the car which can affect their sense of balance coupled with a fear of unfamiliar territory.

As a minimum requirement you will need a secure carrier, but if you have a kitten pen or travelling pen, you can acclimatise your cat to travel in his pen complete with

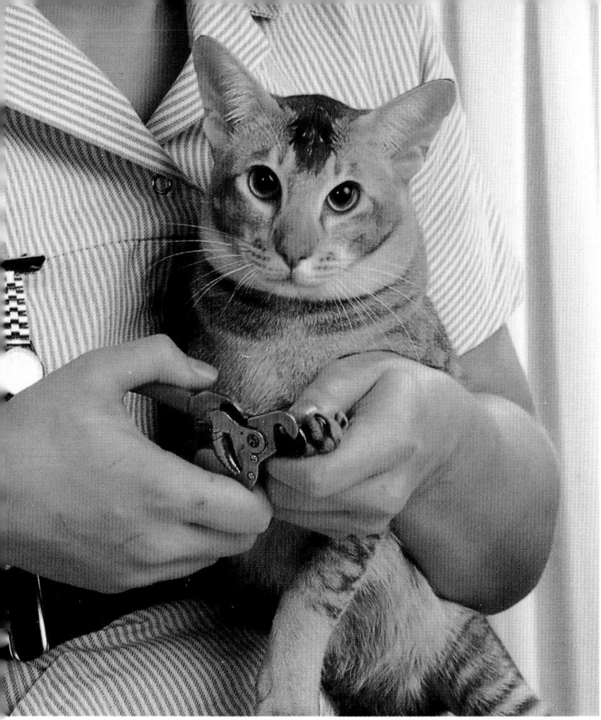

Claw-clipping is an essential part of the grooming routine. This cat has learnt to accept the procedure calmly, knowing that he has nothing to fear.

Photo: Hubert King, W.W. Winter.

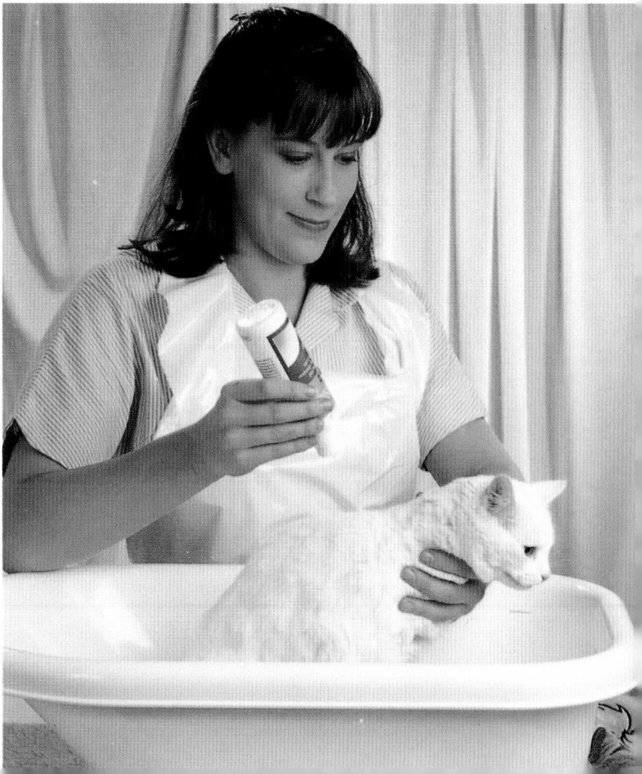

Talk reassuringly to your cat when you are bathing him, and always reward him with his favourite dinner when you have finished.

Photo: Hubert King, W.W. Winter.

Start off by getting your cat used to having his mouth examined, and once this causes no problems, you can progress to cleaning the teeth.

Photo: Hubert King, W.W. Winter.

Your cat will learn to accept ear-cleaning, but make sure you do not probe too deeply into the ear canal as this could cause pain or injury.

Photo: Hubert King, W.W. Winter.

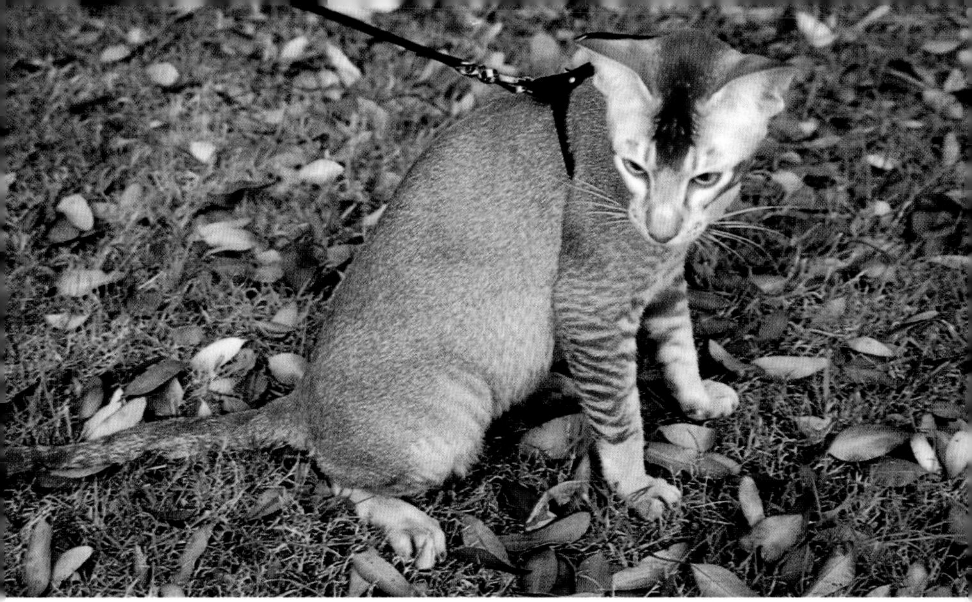

ABOVE: Teaching your cat to walk on a lead requires considerable patience. Food rewards will help your cat to overcome his initial resistance. *Photo: Steve Franklin.*

BELOW: Make the inside of the cat-carrier as comfortable as possible, and use some food rewards to tempt your cat to go into it. Soon he will learn to accept the confinement without protest. *Photo: Hubert King, W.W. Winter.*

If your cat is used to being handled by friends and family, he should not object to being examined by a judge.

Photo: Sally Franklin.

A show cat may be kept ir his pen for relatively long periods. It is important tha he is taught tc settle, and is prevented from becoming destructive.

Photo: Brend Watson

Give your cat a chance to explore the photographer's studio before setting him up to pose for pictures.

Photos: Hubert King, W.W. Winter.

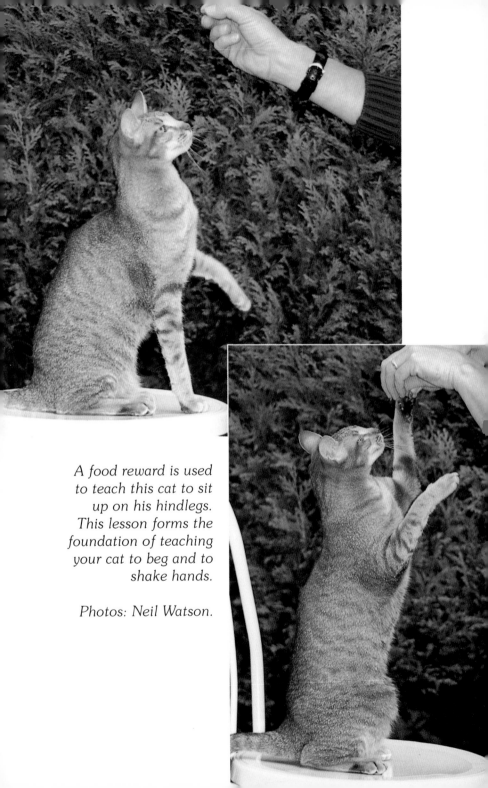

A food reward is used to teach this cat to sit up on his hindlegs. This lesson forms the foundation of teaching your cat to beg and to shake hands.

Photos: Neil Watson.

This cat has learnt to stand on his hindlegs by using a toy as a training aid. Photos: Hubert King, W.W. Winter.

JUMPING THROUGH A HOOP
Photos: Neil Watson.

ABOVE: The cat jumps when given the command, aiming for the food reward that is held out the other side of the hoop.

LEFT. Safe landing – and the cat will immediately receive his reward.

his litter tray. The beauty of this set-up is that it enables your cat to have the freedom to move about within an enclosed space.

EQUIPMENT: Cat carrier, kitten or travelling pen, optional litter tray and water bowls.

TRAINING OBJECTIVE: To enable your cat to travel in his carrier in the car as part of his normal routine, without injury to himself or creating danger for the driver.

TRAINING STEPS
1. Make sure your cat is familiar with and comfortable in his carrier or pen. (See above.)
2. Do not feed your cat before a journey to avoid car-sickness.
3. Take your cat for a short ride in the car. If he shows any sign of being restless after a short journey take him home again.
4. After a couple of days' break, take him for another car ride, of longer duration.
5. Repeat these journeys on a regular basis, making sure that each drive is longer than the last one. You will be able to assess when your cat feels comfortable with the routine and shows no agitation when getting into the car. Reward him by giving affection and treats.

31. TO SETTLE IN A CATTERY

The occasion may arise when you have to put your cat in a cattery. This may be because of holidays or because of illness. Even if you do not see an immediate need for boarding your cat, it is a good idea to find a suitable cattery in your area in case of emergency.

Make sure the cattery is suitably licensed, according to local regulations. The accommodation should be of a reasonable size, clean and dry with a solid, easy-to-clean base. Most outside runs should be housed on a similar base which makes for easy cleaning after each resident has left. Some guidelines also recommend a sneeze barrier between each run to prevent the transmission of infection.

Other factors to check for include the requirement for up-to-date vaccination certificates, the feeding of any special diets, whether any other animals such as dogs or rabbits are boarded on the same premises, security of premises and continuity of care.

EQUIPMENT: Current vaccination card, optional extras – your cat's own food, toys, bedding, and litter.

TRAINING OBJECTIVE: To train your cat to accept his cattery accommodation as his second home.

TRAINING STEPS
1. Train your cat to travel in his cat carrier (see above).
2. Once you have found a cattery that meets your specifications, book your cat to spend one night on the premises. On collection, your cat's demeanour will tell you volumes about what he thinks of his holiday home. It will also give you the chance to assess his living accommodation and on-going care.

3. Increase your cat's sense of familiarity by asking the cattery owner if he can have his own toys, blankets, feeding bowls and litter trays. In most cases, a cattery owner will allow toys and blankets, even if the other items are not permitted.
4. If your cat is fond of a particular food that is not supplied by the cattery owner, ask if you can leave sufficient supplies to cover your cat's stay.
5. When you collect your cat from his cattery, make a fuss of him when you arrive home and feed him his favourite treats. Make sure that you place his belongings in their usual place at home to increase his sense of security.

32. TO BE A MOUSER

Most cat owners will assume that their cat knows how to chase and catch mice, attributing this behaviour to a cat's natural instincts. However, a few cats can actually show fear and even run away from a mouse. If you want your cat to take on the role of mouser, there are ways of encouraging his hunting instinct.

EQUIPMENT: Fishing-rod type of toy, treats.

TRAINING OBJECTIVE: To train your cat to demonstrate feline behaviour, and to exercise himself.

TRAINING STEPS
1. Encourage your cat to sniff and play with a toy mouse or with a few feathers bound together. Lightly spray toy with liquid catnip or sprinkle a few flakes of dried catnip on to the toy. This will enhance acceptability.
2. Once your cat has demonstrated that he will accept his toy, praise him and reward him with his usual treats.
3. Next, attach the toy to a rod and piece of string. Drag the toy around the floor, calling your cat's name at the same time.
4. Using short, jerky movements with the rod, encourage your cat to start pouncing on the toy, which should smell faintly of catnip. The usual treat, reward and praise should be given at this stage.
5. When your cat has mastered jumping on the toy in your home, transfer his training to your garden or an enclosed safe area. Pull the toy behind you as you run the length of your garden, calling your cat to follow you. After running for a few steps, stop to encourage him to pounce on his toy. Wriggle the rod around so it appears the toy is jumping about of its own accord.
6. Gradually lengthen the time between stops, and your cat should soon learn that he has the time and opportunity to grasp his toy. Each time he runs to grasp his toy, praise him with his favourite food treats and a lot of praise.

33. TO ADAPT TO A NEW HOUSE

Moving house is traumatic enough for the human occupants, so imagine what it is like for your cat, who is a territorial animal by nature. Of course, if you are moving into a new home and watching it being built by stages, you can introduce your cat to his new plot of land on weekly visits and build up a sense of familiarity with his new surroundings.

This is where training your cat to walk on a lead comes into its own. If you are having to wait for the previous owners to vacate the house before moving in, then it might be best not to take your cat on regular visits, especially if other cats are in residence. Old properties can also be a source of problems to your cat. Many of these are sold with current certificates identifying preservation treatments, which can be toxic to cats for some time after moving in. These include treatments for woodworm and stains for internal timbers.

EQUIPMENT: A harness or collar, a lead, a cat carrier, blankets, cardboard box(es), catnip, treats.

TRAINING OBJECTIVE: To ease the transition of your cat into his new home in as short a time as possible.

TRAINING STEPS
1. Make sure that your pet is acclimatised to travelling in his carrier before the impending move. (See above.)
2. Restrict your cat on moving day by either locking him into a familiar room with his possessions, or removing him to alternative accommodation that you know he will be happy with.
3. In your new home, transfer your cat's possessions into an 'isolation' room while the removal process is continuing. Provide your cat with a temporary hiding place, a cardboard box with a cut-out cat hole is ideal for this purpose. To make it even more acceptable to your cat, sprinkle a little catnip inside. Do not use a box that has been previously used for storing detergents, bleaches or other household cleaners.
4. Let your cat out into your new home after the removal men have departed. Make sure all windows, external doors and cupboards are closed, including any other potential exit points such as chimneys, and give him the chance to explore his new surroundings, one room at a time at his leisure.
5. Arrange his feeding tray in a similar way to that of his old home, and give him his favourite foods. Some cats show an external reaction to the stress of the move by refusing to eat and drink for a day or so. If your cat reacts in such a way, keep a close eye on him, in the event of an illness developing.
6. Make sure that you give your cat even more affection at this time to see him through the stress of the move.

34. TO LAY CLAIM TO HIS TERRITORY

If your cat is one who spends time outside, you will have to make a decision when to let him out to explore and lay a claim to his new territory. Cats are no respecters of legal boundaries; their boundaries are indicative of the degree of power and confidence they feel within a certain territory.

TRAINING OBJECTIVE: To judge when it is safe to allow your cat out in his new territory – and encourage him to come home again.

TRAINING STEPS
1. Keep your cat inside his new home for at least a week. Some cats show no inclination to go outside for quite a few weeks after a house move – this is not at all unusual.
2. Allow your cat outside when he is really hungry. If necessary, withhold a meal.

This will ensure that he will not travel too far from his home and will respond to the normal call for a meal.
3. Accompany your cat on his first few excursions outside when he will start to lay claim to his new territory by dropping his 'scent markers'.
4. When you feel confident enough to let your cat outside on his own for short periods of time, keep a close watch on his movements, in the event of him meeting another cat in his garden that he has come to adopt as his own territory.

35. TO PREVENT YOUR CAT RETURNING TO HIS FORMER HOME

Sometimes a house move only involves a small change in geography to a cat and, once let out, the cat soon comes across familiar territorial routes leading to his old home. This could mean that your cat has not created his own territory at your new house. In a situation like this, you need to seek the goodwill of your house purchasers to take deterrent action and aid you in training your cat to accept your new home as his new home.

EQUIPMENT
Citrus peel, citrus-based aromatherapy spray or diluted vinegar spray, cat carrier.

TRAINING STEPS
1. Ask your purchasers to take deterrent action by not feeding your cat in his old house or outside territory.
2. Ask them to throw water at him when they see him in his old garden.
3. Attempt to change the smell of the old garden by placing old citrus peel on the ground. Alternatively, obtain a citrus-based aromatherapy spray or diluted vinegar spray to use on the garden.
4. When you collect your cat from his sorties, try and confuse him by taking him home using different routes.
5. If necessary, remove your cat to a cattery well outside his normal geographical area for at least a couple of weeks to help him to forget his old territory.
6. If the attachment to the old house and territory continues, keep your old cat inside your new home for a few weeks. This will probably tax your patience, as he will require your time, love and affection with small but frequent meals served throughout the day to reinforce his links with his new home.
7. When you feel satisfied that your cat's 'homing' instinct is transferred to his new home, follow steps 2-4 of the section entitled "When to let your cat out."

Chapter Five

THE SHOW CAT

Showman or show-stopper – naturally, everybody thinks their cat is the best! If showing your cat is your aim, regardless of whether your cat will compete in the pedigree section or household pet section, you need to commence training in earnest for the big day as soon as possible.

Entering your cat into a show means allowing strangers, dressed in white coats, to handle your pet in a variety of positions and poses. He will also be encouraged to stand on a table top, and will have to cope with strangers looking at him in an enclosed area. Worse of all, if your cat likes an enclosed litter tray, he will be expected to use an open, shallow, small, white litter tray to relieve himself.

36. HOW TO BE A SHOW CAT

In order to look his best, your cat needs to be in the best of health. This means providing a well-balanced, healthy diet, sufficient exercise and an adequate on-going vaccination and worming programme. There are other requirements imposed by the ruling bodies. These include: official registration, minimum age, vaccinations, limitations such as pregnant queens or those who recently kittened, frequency of showing, declawing or other surgical alteration, and defects which preclude showing or winning.

TRAINING OBJECTIVE: To ascertain whether your cat is show material.

TRAINING STEPS

1. Check if your pet has any faults, both obvious and not-so-obvious. Some of these apply both to household pets and pedigree cats, others are designed for pedigree cats only. Examples of faults include kinked tail, squint, 'battle damage', such as scars or torn ears, protruding sternum (breastbone), monorchid or cryptorchid (wrong number of testicles!), undershot or overshot jaws, flat skull or flat chest or undersized for the age of the cat. If you are in any doubt, you should consult with an experienced breeder or your vet.
2. For pedigree cats, check to see how your cat compares to the Standard of Points for his breed, colour and pattern. Showing organisations prepare these as a guide to judges, breeders and exhibitors to describe the points to look for in a breed. Ask an experienced breeder for advice.

37. TO LOOK HIS BEST

Preparation starts as soon as you have entered for the show. As well as the regular grooming and care covered in Chapter Three, special checks need to be made to ensure your cat stands the best chance of winning on the day.

TRAINING OBJECTIVE: To prepare your cat for the show.

TRAINING STEPS
1. Trim your cat's claws regularly. No judge or steward likes to be scratched, however unintentional this is on the cat's behalf.
2. Check your cat's coat for fleas and other small parasites your cat may have acquired. This routine should be part of your cat's general maintenance but make a point of checking at least two weeks before the show, so any necessary remedial action can be taken.
3. Check the ears for wax. Again, this should be part of your cat's on-going maintenance.
4. Check your cat for any possible worm infestation. Cats and kittens should be regularly wormed and you do not want to be embarrassed at a show, if your cat uses his litter tray and there is evidence of worm infestation for other exhibitors and cat show visitors to see.
5. Seek help from your vet if you notice any infections, however minimal. A simple course of antibiotics or long-acting antibiotic injection may do the trick. If not, you may have to resign yourself to missing your day out at the show and forfeiting your show fees.
6. Keep your cat's coat in the peak of show condition by regular grooming.

38. TO BEHAVE AT CAT SHOWS

This is where the fun begins! In fact the training required for showing is all part of a socialisation process which all cats would benefit from – and they certainly enjoy the extra treats and toys which are used in training.

EQUIPMENT: You will need to obtain a suitable cat pen, and the necessary show equipment, so that your pet is familiar with them before the show.

TRAINING OBJECTIVE: To acclimatise your pet to stay inside the pen for relatively long periods. The minimum time your cat will be penned at a show will be 6-7 hours and, in Europe and America, shows can last for more than one day. Your cat will also have to get used to wearing a piece of ribbon or elastic around his neck, which will be used to display his pen number on a disc.

TRAINING STEPS
1. Set up your pen on the table and prepare its interior as described under your registration body's show rules. For the beginning of the training session, use your cat's own familiar blankets, a small open litter tray, water and food bowls.
2. Place your cat into the pen for a short period of time. Reward him with a food treat when removing him from his pen.
3. Gradually increase the length of time on a daily basis. It is a good idea to place some of your cat's favourite toys in the pen – although this will not be permitted on show days.
4. Tie a piece of ribbon or some elastic around your cat's neck so that he gets used

to wearing it. Watch him carefully for a few sessions to ensure that he does not trap one of his legs as he tries to remove the ribbon or elastic or choke on whatever you have tied around his neck. Each time you remove your cat from the pen, take off his ribbon or piece of elastic and reward him with a food treat.

39. TO BE EXAMINED BY A JUDGE

Judges vary greatly in the ways they handle cats. Therefore, the more friends you can persuade to aid you in this process, the better training it provides for the cat. Make sure that your friends carry out adequate disinfection procedures before handling your cat to prevent the transmission of any infection or disease.

TRAINING OBJECTIVE: To get your cat used to being handled by a variety of people.

TRAINING STEPS

1. Encourage your friends to pick up your cat and talk to him in a gentle voice. Reward your cat with his favourite food treat at the end of each session.
2. Familiarise your cat to get used to his body being held in various poses. Generally, a steward will extract the cat from his pen by the rear end. The cat is then placed on the judge's table. The judge or steward will pick up the cat again, and, while raising him, stretch out his whole body for examination. After this has been completed to the judges' satisfaction, the cat is placed on the table, or held with just his back paws resting on the judging table. Practise all these manoeuvres while gently speaking to, and encouraging, your cat. Reward your cat with his food treats after handling.
3. Lift up his lip so that he gets used to someone looking at his teeth. The alignment of the cat's lower and upper jaw is checked at the same time, although this usually applies to pedigree show entrants only. Many cats become frightened when being handled in this way, so take training slowly, encouraging your cat at all stages. After each attempt, reward with a favourite food treat.
5. When your cat is used to being handled by you and your friends, introduce a white coat into the scenario. Familiarise your cat with seeing you and your friends wearing this coat, and with being handled by white-coated people. At the end of each session, bring out the usual food reward treat.
6. Find a small table, and protect its surface from cat scratches. Place your cat on its surface so he is used to being confined to a small space by a white-coated person. When each session has finished, reward with the food treat.

40. NOT TO WRECK THE SHOW PEN

When visiting a show, it is not unusual to see at least one show pen destroyed, with the pen number card dragged through the bars of the pen and chewed or torn by the pen's inmate. Many visitors are amused at such antics, but it can indicate that the cat inside the pen is most unhappy at being confined for such a long period of time.

TRAINING OBJECTIVE: To settle happily inside the pen and not to be destructive.

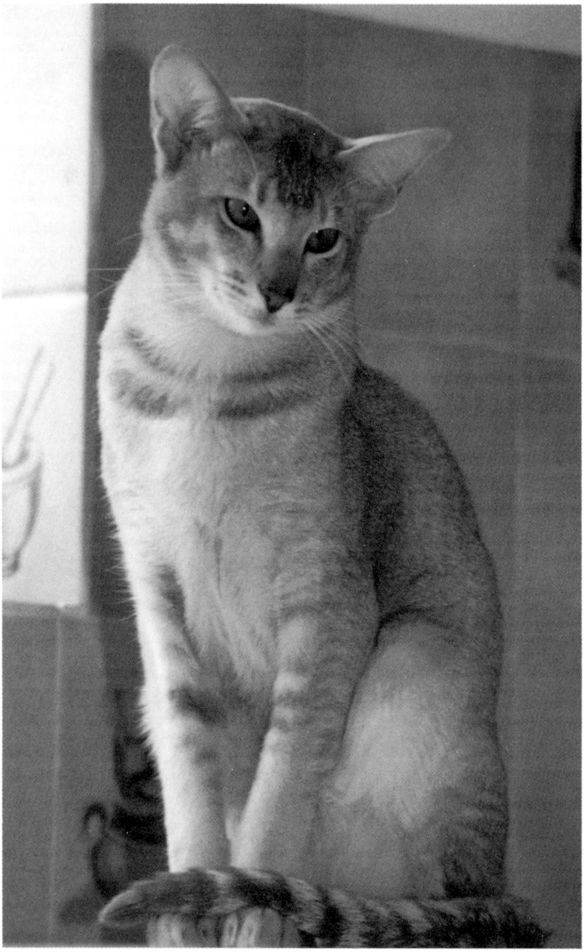

Toffee: Posing to perfection.

Photo: Steve Franklin.

TRAINING STEPS

1. Attach a piece of paper on the outside of your makeshift show pen at home. This is in place of the pen number card that is used at shows. Also try pinning a small rosette to the outside of the pen. If your cat attempts to pull the paper or rosette through the bars of his pen, spray him with water and say the word "No". Do not reward this behaviour with a food treat.

2. If your cat attempts to sweep the contents of his litter tray on to the floor of the pen, tell him "No" in a loud firm voice, and use your water spray. Help your cat by using less litter, and a slightly higher-sided litter tray. If the litter stays intact in the litter tray, praise your cat and reward him with his favourite treats.

4. If your cat attempts to sprinkle water from his drinking bowl over the contents of

his makeshift show pen, change his bowl to a D-shaped cup that has wire hangers. This can be attached to the pen at a height where your cat cannot spill it. If you cannot get hold of this type of cup, try using a bowl that is weighted at the bottom. Also try pouring less water into the drinking bowl – you can always add more during show day.

5. Your cat may try to burrow under his blankets, thereby upsetting other items of his show kit. Some owners cure this problem by purchasing an extra blanket to make a cover, one corner of which is suspended from the top of the pen, for the cat to hide behind. Speak to your cat kindly when he is hiding behind his blanket so he does not become withdrawn.

You may have to accept that sometimes a cat indicates his unhappiness by wrecking his pen, however much training or remedial work you undertake. In some cases, it is better to give up this type of training, and not subject your cat to show conditions.

41. TO POSE FOR PHOTOGRAPHS

Unfortunately, you cannot recreate some of the funniest things your cat does for the camera – but your pet can be trained to behave and pose in front of a photographer. Some cats will pose quite happily at home for their owners, though it becomes a different matter when they are taken to a studio.

TRAINING OBJECTIVE: To encourage your cat to pose for photographs in an unfamiliar environment.

TRAINING STEPS

1. Calm your cat down after his journey to the studio. Sit him on your knee, check his appearance and lightly groom his coat. Give him a food treat as his reward.
2. With the agreement of the photographer, let your cat explore the studio.
3. Place your cat on the table or chair provided. To begin with, he will want to jump off and explore, but be patient and soon he will realise that the chair or table is the scene of the action.
4. Check with the photographer, and then sprinkle a *minute* quantity of dried catnip on the table or chair. Alternatively use a light spray of liquid catnip from an aerosol can. Do not use too much or your cat may be photographed in a drunken stupor, instead of showing a lively, intelligent expression.
5. Listen to your photographer's instructions regarding the use of toys and the calling of your cat's name. Hopefully, your cat will soon forget the bright lights and clicking noises as he jumps around on the chair or table to attack some imaginary bird in flight. Often, the best photograph is one of the earliest in the sequence when your cat is at his most alert, showing a lively interest in his new surroundings.

Chapter Six

CLEVER CATS

Many people think it is impossible to train a cat to perform tricks, but when you think about it, large cats have been trained to perform tricks in circuses for hundreds of years. You know your cat has intelligence and some degree of learning capability. While this may not enable your cat to graduate with a degree in Feline Studies, you can harness a little of the cat's independent streak and train him to perform tricks, such as sitting, sitting-up, shaking hands, rolling over and jumping through a hoop on command. Who knows, next stop Hollywood!

Success will need to be reinforced with very tasty food treats – after all, training your cat to perform tricks is not a function of a cat's natural behaviour. He will want to perform these tricks because it is fun for him and a very creative form of communication between cat and owner. All training should be carried out in a quiet location, without any form of interruption.

Trials have shown that a cat of average ability can learn these tricks in approximately ten lessons. Some cats will learn faster, others will take longer. Success is also down to your skill as the trainer, your perception of your cat's abilities, your success in communicating your commands, and the degree of physical prompting you may have to use initially. While training, you will need to sit in front of your cat to speak to him, and show him certain actions.

42. HOW TO SIT

Responding to the command "Sit" forms the basis for the additional tricks of shaking hands, sitting-up and begging.

TRAINING OBJECTIVE: To sit on command.

TRAINING STEPS

1. Take your cat to the required location, such as a stool, a chair or a table. Make sure the chosen item has easy access for the cat. Show your cat the item you would like him to sit on.
2. With a food treat in your hand, place your cat on the stool. Show him the treat as you say "Sit".
3. Your cat's response will probably be to either jump up to your hand or stand up on his hind legs to reach the food treat.
4. Place your hand on his rump and push him down. Say the word, "Sit". Your cat may react with a miaow or jump off the stool. He will certainly be puzzled in the early stages of training.

This 16-year-old cat has been trained to sit up and beg for his treats.

Photo: Steve Franklin.

5. Repeat steps 2 - 4 a few times. If you have succeeded in getting your cat to sit at the end of the lesson, say the word "Good", give him his treat and lots of praise. You may have to repeat this training session over a few days. Some cats will catch on at the end of one day's training, other cats will need their training to be reinforced over a few days.

43. TO SIT UP ON HINDLEGS

This trick builds on the cat's instincts to grasp out for an object held above his head.

TRAINING OBJECTIVE: To teach your cat to sit up on his hindlegs when instructed.

TRAINING STEPS

1. Command your cat to sit.
2. Say the word "Up", and hold a food treat above the cat's head. Your cat will respond by standing up and grasping upwards for the treat.
3. Give the command to sit again, and give the treat as soon as your cat balances, sitting on his hind legs. What you are actually doing is monitoring his behaviour so he gets the idea that the word "Up" means sitting up, as opposed to reaching up or standing up.
4. Remember to say the word "Good" when he responds correctly, and praise him as well.

44. TO BEG

This is another variation based on the "sit up on hindlegs sequence" – and we have even seen it used as a prelude to grooming your cat! The same training steps can be used whether you decide to train your cat using a table or using the floor as a base.

TRAINING OBJECTIVE: To beg for treats on command.

TRAINING STEPS

1. Command your cat to sit.
2. Hold the food in one hand, slightly out of reach, above his head. If you have decided to use 'wet' food as your motivator, place it on a spoon.
3. Say the word "Up", and slowly raise your spoon or hand up and away from you. Your cat will reach to touch your hand or spoon with one or both paws. At this juncture say the word "Beg". As he reaches for the food, he will automatically adopt the "beg" position, with his front paws hanging down as he bends the carpal bones in his front legs.
4. You need to keep him in the begging position for a few seconds and give him his reward. Say the word "Good", and remember to praise him while he is still in the begging position.
5. Repeat steps 1 to 5 over several sessions a day, for a period of at least a week, until he learns the desired behaviour. Your cat must learn to associate that the begging position means an instant reward of a treat. If you give him the treat when he has dropped to his normal 'all-fours' position, he will not make the correct association.
6. Carry on repeating this trick, but start removing the cue of food treats so that he learns to associate your hand with the required response. Always finish the training session with a food treat.

45. TO SHAKE HANDS

This trick is usually mastered quite quickly. There is no doubt that this is a good way to impress visitors to your home!

TRAINING OBJECTIVE: To shake hands on command.

TRAINING STEPS

1. Instruct your cat to sit.
2. Say the word "Shake" and pick up one of your cat's front paws.
3. Say the word "Good", praise him and give him a food treat.
4. Repeat steps 1 to 3 a few times, always with the same paw. End the session before your cat's attention turns to something else. You may find that during the first training session, your cat will, after a few attempts, lift his paw up on his own. When this occurs, praise him well and give him more food treats.

46. TO RETRIEVE

Cats can be taught to retrieve items, such as paper-balls and catnip toys. Some moggies and indeed a few pedigree breeds, such as Orientals and Siamese, show an innate predisposition to retrieve without any form of training.

TRAINING OBJECTIVE: To retrieve the toy that is thrown by the owner.

EQUIPMENT: A small flat-shaped toy (preferably without a squeak).

TRAINING STEPS
Training Session I
1. Instruct your cat to sit and stay.
2. Place the toy in front of your cat. He will probably lean forward to sniff it, especially if you have smeared it with something tasty, such as freshly cooked chicken juice. As soon as you see him show an interest in the toy, praise him and give him a treat.
3. If your cat has not moved away, encourage him to put his head forward again to sniff the toy. As soon as he has done this, encourage his efforts with more praise and another treat.
4. If your cat has moved away after the first attempt, bring him back to you, instruct him to sit and encourage him to sniff the object. Reinforce again with praise and food treats. This part of training should take approximately a week, with training sessions built into the day on a regular basis.

Training Session II
5. As soon as the cat has learnt that sniffing the toy results in a treat, the routine will need to be changed to encourage him to sniff without receiving his reward. This is done by smearing the toy with his favourite food.
6. As soon as your cat puts his mouth over the toy or stick, say the words "Pick it up", so that he will associate the words with picking up the toy or stick. When this step is complete, praise him and offer him his food reward.
7. Repeat Step 6 on a regular basis.

Training Session III
8. As soon as your cat has mastered placing the toy in his mouth, smother it again with his favourite food and throw it a few inches away from your cat. Say the words "Pick it up". He will be drawn to the toy by its smell and will attempt to put his mouth around it again. When he does this, praise him and offer him more food rewards. Repeat this step on a regular basis as well.

Training Session IV
9. When it is clear that Step 8 has been mastered, throw the toy and say the words "Pick it up". When he does this, praise him well. The idea is to get him used to the idea of picking up the object without receiving his food reward. When this part of the training session is complete, there is only one more stage to complete.

Training Session V
10. To complete this trick, call your cat by his name to return to you when he has the toy in his mouth.
11. As soon as he completes this action, remove the toy from him, praise him and reward him with his favourite food treats.
12. Repeat Steps 9 - 11 on a regular basis, throughout the day, over a period of at least a week. On average, it takes four to five weeks to train your cat to carry out

this trick. The key is to follow the training steps on a regular pattern, throughout the day, over a period of at least a week for each session.

47. TO LIE DOWN

This particular trick does not rely on the behaviours that have been taught in the previous sequence of tricks. We are training the cat in a new foundation behaviour that can be built on for the next trick. This particular trick differs from the trick of sitting on command, which requires very little physical intervention. This one involves more hands-on intervention from the trainer.

TRAINING OBJECTIVE: To instruct your cat to lie down on his side.

TRAINING STEPS

1. Say the word "Down", and gently push your cat down and off his feet.
2. While pushing your cat down, keep on repeating the word "Down" in a firm but gentle voice.
3. When you feel the resistance ceasing, gently push your cat over on to his side to lie down. Say the word "Good", reward him with food treats and lots of praise. When you initially push your cat down you will be aware of his body resisting your pushing efforts. Do not move your hand in a stroking motion, keep your hand in one position over his body as you push him down. Your first attempt may result in your cat attempting to run away from you, so when you start pushing, use your other hand to steady him for a few seconds and then lift it off.
4. When your cat is down on his side, say the word "Stay", and reward him with his food treats.
5. The training sequence covering Steps 1 to 4, will need to be reinforced, probably over a few lessons. The aim is to train him by using one hand only to do the pushing movement at this stage.
6. After these training steps have been carried out a few times, you will notice your cat will show less resistance to your hand. It is important to keep praising him and offering him food treats each time he lies down for you.
7. You will soon reach the stage that as you say "Down", you will simply have to hold your hand out and your cat will lie down, without any physical prompting.

48. TO ROLL OVER

With this trick, you are extending the skills your cat has learned in lying down to command.

TRAINING OBJECTIVE: To teach your cat to lie down and roll over to his opposite side on command.

TRAINING STEPS

1. Instruct your cat to lie down by saying "Down".
2. Holding a treat in front of his nose, say "Roll over", and move the hand containing the treat over the cat's head. The cat's head and body will instinctively follow your hand and your cat will roll over.
3. It is most unusual if the cat's head does not follow what his nose is smelling. However, if this does not happen, roll his body over. Once your cat has achieved a

roll over, give the treat and plenty of praise.
4. Steps 1 - 3 will need to be carried out quite a few times for reinforcement. Gradually, you will be able to move your hand further away from the cat's nose. In time, he will learn that a semi-circular movement from your hand means roll over.

49. TO JUMP THROUGH A HOOP

We are now moving away from the idea of using a base trick which can be used as the foundation behaviour for a further series of tricks. This particular trick involves a different sequence of actions from your cat, commencing at floor level. In fact, this is a very simple trick to teach your cat. One word of caution: remove any valuable ornaments – you may knock them over in your enthusiasm!

TRAINING OBJECTIVE: To teach your cat to jump through a hoop on command.

EQUIPMENT: Fluorescent coloured hula-hoops are available, or you can make your own from plastic tubing bought from your local Do-it-Yourself supermarket or store.

TRAINING STEPS
1. Hold your hoop vertically on the floor, call your cat's name and encourage him to walk through the hoop. As he gets near the hoop say the word "Jump". Immediately he has walked through the hoop, offer him a treat.
2. Repeat Step 1 a few times, until you are satisfied that your cat has learned the sequence.
3. Repeat Step 1, but raise the hoop slightly from the floor. When your cat walks close to the hoop, say the word "Jump", and when he responds correctly, give him the usual treat and praise.
4. When your cat is happy with walking through a raised hoop, repeat Step 1, gradually raising the hoop to different heights until he perceives he can no longer walk through it. Encourage your cat to jump through the hoop by saying the word "Jump".
5. At this point, your cat may decide to walk around the hoop or scrabble underneath it. If this happens, withhold the treats and praise.
4. Reinforce Step 4, using a height your cat is comfortable with. Once this step has been reinforced, you should be able to raise the hoop even higher. After this trick has been mastered, you can train your cat to jump back through the hoop.

50. TO SWIM

Contrary to popular belief, some cats do have a fascination and even an affinity for water, whether it drips out of a tap or sits reflecting sunlight in the washing-up bowl. It is well known that cats when faced with danger on water will swim away from the source. The well-known Turkish Van love water and there are many photographs of these cats enjoying a dip in the bath, especially on a hot day.

With this trick it is important to choose a cat who is out-going by nature, and who is fascinated by water. It is counter-productive, and most unkind, to select a cat that shows fear or even an aversion to water.

Make sure the water is at the correct temperature to avoid your cat getting cold. Also check that the temperature in the room is adequate; you do not want to bring your cat out of warm water into a cold room. Obviously, do not put bubble-bath or any other scented product into the water. After the swimming session, dry your cat thoroughly.

TRAINING OBJECTIVE: To encourage your cat to swim in the bath.

TRAINING STEPS

Training Session I

1. Fill your bath to a depth of a couple of inches, using lukewarm water. Gently lower your swimmer into the water and encourage him to walk around in the water, without losing his balance.
2. Speak to him constantly, praise him and offer him his food treats.
3. Remove him from the bath and make sure he is dried thoroughly. His body should feel warm to your touch. If your cat is let out while damp, he could catch a nasty cold.
4. Repeat Steps 1 - 3 over a period of a few days so your cat will associate paddling with extra special food treats and praise from his owner.

Training Session II

5. When your cat is comfortable with this depth of water, increase the depth by another few inches, or to the depth you feel he can handle comfortably. Stay with him all the time, offering encouragement, praise and food treats.
6. Repeat Step 5 a few times until you feel he is comfortable with his surroundings and depth of water. Dry him thoroughly when removing him from the bath.

Training Session III

7. Fill the bath to a level that will support your cat's body comfortably. Lower him into the water and, supporting him, move him gently through the water. Talk to him all the time, praising his efforts. He will instinctively move his legs in a paddling motion. Remove him from the bath, dry him thoroughly and offer him his food treats.
8. Repeat Step 7 a few times until you feel your cat is comfortable with the situation, and with the depth of water.

Training Session IV

9. Fill the bath to the level that your cat is happy with, and lower him gently into the water. Support him for a few swimming exercises, and then try letting go of him to swim a few inches on his own. When he achieves this milestone, give lots of praise. Remove him from the bath and dry him thoroughly. Give him the most succulent of food treats as his reward.

CONCLUSION

By now, I hope you have trained your cat to achieve a level of performance that is acceptable to you, the owner. In doing this, you will experience a greatly enriched relationship with your feline companion because your cat knows how to please you – and you will also enjoy showing off his tricks to your friends and family. Whatever level of training you achieve, remember your cat is your friend for life – and I wish you a long and happy relationship together.